*The Yale Ben Jonson*

GENERAL EDITORS: ALVIN B. KERNAN AND RICHARD B. YOUNG

Woodcut illustrating the Life of Tiberius, from Suetonius' *Lives of the Twelve Caesars*, with commentary by Filippo Beroaldo (Venice, 1610).

# Ben Jonson: Sejanus

EDITED BY JONAS A. BARISH

NEW HAVEN AND LONDON:
YALE UNIVERSITY PRESS

# Contents

# Preface of the General Editors

The Yale edition of the plays of Ben Jonson is intended to meet two fundamental requirements: first, the need of the modern reader for a readily intelligible text which will convey, as nearly as an edition can, the life and movement which invests the plays on the stage; second, the need of the critic and scholar for a readily available text which represents as accurately as possible, though it does not reproduce, the plays as Jonson printed them. These two requirements are not, we believe, incompatible, but the actual adjustment of one to the other has been determined by the judgment of the individual editors. In details of editorial practice, therefore, the individual volumes of the edition may vary, but in basic editorial principle they are consistent.

The texts are based primarily on the two folio volumes of Jonson's *Works*, the first published in 1616, the second in 1640. The 1616 volume was seen through the press by Jonson himself, and therefore represents to a degree unusual for dramatic texts of the period what the dramatist intended us to have. The 1640 volume presents more difficult textual problems; though Jonson himself began preparing individual plays for it as early as 1631, these were carelessly printed—a fact of which he was painfully aware—and the folio, under the editorship of the eccentric Sir Kenelm Digby, was not completed until after Jonson's death. The quarto editions have also been consulted, and where a quarto reading has been preferred by an editor the necessary information appears in the notes.

In editing Jonson for the modern reader, one of the central problems is that of annotation, a problem that is complicated rather than solved by providing a catalogue of Jonson's immense classical learning or of his contemporary lore. We have believed that annotation is most helpful not when it identifies or defines details but when it clarifies the context of the detail. Consequently, citation of sources, allusions, and analogues, whether classical or colloquial, has been controlled by and restricted to what is relevant in the judgment of the editors to a meaningful understanding of the dramatic and poetic values of the passage in question and of the play as a whole. For the same reason, all editorial apparatus—introductions, notes, and glosses—frequently and deliberately deal with critical and interpretative matters in order to reanimate the topical details and give substance to the imaginative world each play creates.

To provide a readable text it has been necessary to revise some of the printing conventions of the seventeenth-century editions. In order to identify himself with the classical tradition of comedy, Jonson used as a model for his *Works* the first printed editions of Plautus, Terence, and Aristophanes, heading each scene with a list of all characters appearing in it, without marking individual entrances and exits. The present edition follows the more familiar practice of listing only those characters on stage at the beginning of a scene and indicates all entrances and exits. Stage directions, kept to an absolute minimum, have also been added where understanding of the dialogue depends on an implied but not explicit action, or on an unspecified location. With the exception of the first speech ascription in each scene, which is usually omitted by Jonson, all such additions and all material not in the original text have been enclosed in square brackets.

Where Jonson printed all verse in the metrical unit of the line, whether or not it represents the speech of one or more than one character, this edition divides the parts of such lines according to the speaker, and indicates the metrical unit by echeloning the parts of the line.

The original punctuation has been followed where its rhetorical effect has a dramatic value, but modern pointing has been used wherever necessary to clarify syntactical obscurities and to eliminate obvious errors or mere eccentricity. Spelling has been modernized except where orthographical change affects either meaning or meter. For example, where Jonson prints *'d* to indicate an unstressed ending of a past participle, this edition prints *-ed*, and where Jonson printed *-ed* to indicate stress this edition prints *-èd*. Jonson's frequent elisions, e.g. *th'* or *i'*, are retained, and all unusual accents are marked.

In the original text the entrance of a new character usually, though not invariably, initiates a new scene, so that there are many more scenes than a fully modernized text would allow. This edition retains Jonson's act and scene divisions in the belief that in most cases they represent the linking effect, the *liaison des scènes*, characteristic of the developing neoclassic drama; in all cases they represent Jonson's own conception of dramatic form; and the fact of form is part of the meaning of his plays.

Retaining the original act and scene divisions means that the act and scene numbers of the Yale Ben Jonson correspond to those of the standard edition of Jonson, edited by C. H. Herford and Percy and Evelyn Simpson (11 vols. Oxford, 1925–52). This enables the reader to consult with ease the notes of Herford and Simpson, who list classical sources and analogues, and to refer without difficulty to the original text. Line numbers in brackets indicate the lineation of Herford and Simpson.

# Introduction

*Sejanus His Fall* belongs to that small band of plays destined to survive mainly as "closet" drama, yet paradoxically owing their survival to the fact of having been conceived for the stage. Of plays meant for reading, only *Samson Agonistes* and (to a lesser extent) *Prometheus Unbound* have managed to surmount the anomaly of having been cast in play form yet not designed for the theater. Plays by the other Romantic and Victorian poets, usually composed in bookish imitation of the Greeks or the Elizabethans, whether intended for performance or not, have long since achieved the oblivion they deserve; so have the academic imitations of Seneca penned by the Countess of Pembroke and her circle during the decade prior to *Sejanus*; and so also have the later, still essentially academic exercises of writers like Addison and Dr. Johnson. *Sejanus* had its first performance in 1603 by the ranking theatrical troupe of the day, the King's Men, at the Globe Theatre; Shakespeare, who acted in it, may have played the part of Tiberius. Despite these good auspices the play did not prosper. Its first audience disliked it vehemently, and it has been little performed since. Nevertheless, it is largely the fact of belonging to a live theatrical tradition, of having been composed by an experienced playwright for an active playing company—as well as by a profound scholar with extraordinary intellectual powers—that make it not just another wooden closet drama, another *Cato* or *Irene*, but one of the neglected masterpieces of the English stage.

The academic Senecan drama of the late sixteenth and early seventeenth centuries, practiced by a group of enthusiastic but largely untalented writers, tended to shun contact with the professional stage. Its exponents wished to write not plays but dramatic poems, after the manner of Seneca himself or of his sixteenth-century French disciples. They cultivated as virtues the peculiar airlessness of Senecan drama, its plotlessness and placelessness, and they filled up the void in its arid geometry with the rhetoric learned from the same source—with Gargantuan monologues, choruses, and passages of stichomythy and aphorism. They leaned markedly toward the topic of statecraft, often turning out plays that were little more than political expositions in dialogue form. In this preoccupation, if in nothing else, they resembled the writers of chronicle history for the public stage. The latter also were devoted to the theme of kingship, but less as a subject of meditation than as a pretext for spectacles, battles, and theatrical sensation. If the academic Senecans carried their interest in "form" to a pedantic extreme, ending in a sterile pseudo-formalism, the popular playwrights often seemed to be successfully imitating the shape of chaos.

*Sejanus* attempts valiantly to mediate between these extremes. Jonson wishes to ruminate on questions of authority and empire, but to do so theatrically, within the confines of plot and character. He wishes to write a "true poem," or authentic tragedy, following the best academic authorities on the subject, but to do so for the public theater—to please and instruct unlettered audiences without falling into the promiscuous sensationalism of the chronicle play. He tries, hence, to incorporate into his play the significant virtues of both kinds of drama, the dignity and eloquence of the one, the vividness and direct impact of the other. In the effort to discipline and chasten his material, he does not scruple to adopt the rhetorical techniques of Senecan tragedy, the formal narratives in which offstage action is described or past history recapitulated, the colloquies of debate on politics and power, the weighty monologues on the same subject, the *sententiae* with which characters give epigrammatic density to their views, and even an approximation of a chorus in the group of bystanders who comment on the action as it unfolds.

At the same time, Jonson conducts his plot as a seasoned man of the theater, mindful of the need for narrative tension, stage movement, and physical confrontation of character with character. He bows to the Elizabethan taste for spectacle and stage violence. From his historical sources he chooses incidents that lend themselves to dramatic treatment, and he does not hesitate to rearrange history when rearrangement will heighten the theatrical impact without deforming the ethical design. Thus the trial scene in Act III combines three separate meetings of the Senate, one involving the presentation of the sons of Germanicus, another the trial of Silius, a third the arraignment of Cordus.

In one respect, however, *Sejanus* constitutes a radical departure from both traditions—in its generally extraordinary fidelity to its sources. It probably marks the most complete attempt ever made to follow the dictates of Italian Renaissance critics, who had judged history to be the only proper basis for a tragedy. Behind this odd prescription lay the belief that the effect of catharsis—the arousing and allaying of the passions—could best be accomplished when the spectator knew that the strange and terrible events he was witnessing had actually happened. Aristotle himself had led the way on this point, declaring that what convinces us is the possible, and that we naturally believe in the possibility of an action if we know that it has in fact taken place.

But neither the academic Senecans, nor, certainly, the writers of chronicle plays had ever regarded themselves as more than casually bound to history. They pillaged anecdotes from Plutarch or elsewhere and proceeded to dramatize them as they pleased, adding, cutting, splicing, and transposing at every step. *Sejanus* displays an unwonted attentiveness to the history it follows, and it follows *all* its sources. To the writing of his play Jonson brought a scholar's command of the historical materials, and a scholar's conscience in dealing with them. He never idly or carelessly departs from the known facts. He never negligently admits anachronisms. He enriches his narrative with authentic detail culled from sources contemporary with the historians themselves. His play thus constitutes in itself a piece of historiography. It offers something like an archaeological reconstruction of the epoch it deals with, and a fully worked out interpretation of its subject, arrived at through a consideration of all relevant evidence. In the process, by the very minuteness of his re-creation, Jonson reveals the nature of his commitment: not to catharsis, not to pity or terror, but to a moral evaluation of history based on a solid and accurate transcription of that history. His objective is moral truth conveyed through historical truth. The same preoccupation with observed fact that in comedy leads Jonson to delight in the picturesque detail, the graphic allusion, the pungent phrase overheard and recorded, in tragedy leads him to his scrupulous adherence to historical particulars. As the most authoritative recent critic of Jonson's intentions in this matter has put it, Jonson is attempting, in effect, to import into the drama the traditional functions of history.[1]

---

1. Joseph Allen Bryant, Jr., "The Significance of Ben Jonson's First Requirement for Tragedy: 'Truth of Argument,'" *Studies in Philology*, 49 (1952), 205. This entire article (pp. 195–213), together with another by Bryant, "*Catiline* and the Nature of Jonson's Tragic Fable," *PMLA*, 69 (1954), 265–77, make up the most important expositions to date of Jonson's tragedies in their relations to history. The present discussion is greatly indebted to both, as also—even when in disagreement—to a third by

But though it is history of a high order, *Sejanus* is first of all a play. Jonson, indeed, would seem to be making in it a nearly unique claim—to be fulfilling simultaneously the offices of historian and poet. The two functions had been sharply discriminated by Sidney, to the disadvantage of history. All human learning, says Sidney in a familiar passage in the *Apology for Poetry*, has as its aim the bringing of men to perfection. Perfection, however, must manifest itself in action; learning aims not merely at "well knowing" but "well doing," and the test for any kind of knowledge is how successfully it serves this end. Of the three chief contenders for top honors, one, says Sidney, philosophy, offers us precept without example, mere empty generality, which never suffices to spur men to deeds. History, on the other hand, especially of the antiquarian sort, gives us example without precept. It shows men in action, but fails to make those actions significant, and so fails to instill into us, as readers, a longing to perform significant actions ourselves. Only the peerless poet "coupleth the generall notion with the particular example."[2] Only the poet offers images of heroic action in a context that stamps them as types of ideal behavior for imitation.

History, moreover, falls short of poetry in another respect. Not only does it fail to provide precepts to accompany its examples, it gives us examples that are themselves ambiguous, hence untrustworthy.

---

Bryant, "The Nature of the Conflict in Jonson's *Sejanus*," *Vanderbilt Studies in the Humanities*, *1* (1951), 197–219. On the relations between history and tragedy, see further B. Giovannini, "Historical Realism and the Tragic Emotions in Renaissance Criticism," *Philological Quarterly*, *32* (1953), 304–20.

2. G. Gregory Smith, ed., *Elizabethan Critical Essays, 1* (Oxford, 1904), 164.

> If the Poet doe his part a-right, he will shew you in *Tantalus,*
> *Atreus,* and such like, nothing that is not to be shunned; in *Cyrus,*
> *Aeneas, Vlisses,* each thing to be followed; where the Historian,
> bound to tell things as things were, cannot be liberall (without hee
> will be poeticall) of a perfect patterne, but, as in *Alexander* or *Scipio*
> himselfe, shew dooings, some to be liked, some to be misliked.
> And then how will you discerne what to followe but by your
> owne discretion, which you had without reading *Quintus Curtius?*
>
> [p. 168]

The historian's very fidelity to fact thus undermines the soundness
of his work as moral example. In the depiction of real persons he
must show you human nature with all its inconsistencies, but
those whose acts are inconsistent can scarcely be taken as models
for emulation. After you have read about Alexander or Scipio
in the chronicles, you must still decide which of their acts to
approve and imitate, which to condemn and avoid; on this point
the historian gives no help. The poet, by contrast, may invent
characters whose every gesture reflects perfection. For Sidney
complexity of characterization in literature is thus clearly not
desirable, but a vice: it introduces unwelcome uncertainties; it
saps the power of fictional characters to inspire worthy acts.
And we should suspect that Sidney speaks for his day, that our
own criterion of psychological complexity, derived mainly from
Shakespeare, finds sanction only in Shakespeare. Shakespeare
aside, the preferred character in Renaissance literature is the
*exemplary* character, in whom the ambiguities and contradictions
found in real persons have been strained out.

Jonson, though he shared Sidney's high regard for poetry,
also venerated history. He lived on terms of friendship with the
leading historians of the day, took an active interest in their work,
and aspired to be of their number; among the manuscripts that
burned in his library fire in 1623 was a nearly completed history
of the reign of Henry V. Sidney had derided the traditional

claims of the historian; Jonson endorses them all. His commendatory verses to Sir Walter Ralegh's *History of the World* extol the historian's labors: history, declares Jonson, is "Times witnesse, herald of Antiquitie, / The light of Truth, and life of Memorie."[3] History, then, binds the human community together in time. It gives men a collective memory; it imposes standards of truth and judgment. Jonson's notion of truth indeed ran more pragmatically to "old Mouse-eaten records" than Sidney's. Jonson had more of the scholar's respect for fact, the scientist's interest in data that could be sifted and verified. In Sidney's view the poet, because of his greater efficacy as a moral teacher, very nearly made the historian unnecessary, and for him the great historians, like Xenophon, were great in precisely the degree to which they contrived to be poets first and antiquaries second. The historian, indeed, with his *lumpen*, positivistic skills, his amassing and recording of data, seemed to Sidney a threat, a rival to the poet with his mythmaking faculty. For Jonson, it would seem, poetry does not invalidate history; rather it completes and perfects it. History shows us what men have in fact done; poetry, purifying history of its blemishes, shows us what they might have done and should have done— what we, moreover, must do in analogous circumstances.

That Jonson took *Sejanus* seriously as history is plain from the extensive marginal notes he affixed to the Quarto text of the play. This was probably the first time that a work of imaginative literature had come forth buttressed with all the apparatus of critical scholarship; the fact suggests the urgency with which Jonson sought to reunite the two ancient and honorable disciplines, both of which he revered. He found his material mainly in Tacitus, secondarily in Suetonius and Dio Cassius, and also in

---

3. C. H. Herford and Percy and Evelyn Simpson, eds., *Ben Jonson*, 8 (Oxford, 1925–52), 176.

multitudes of scattered passages in other writers. Chroniclers of imperial Rome had dwelt with astonishment on the career of Lucius Aelius Sejanus, Tiberius' commander of the guard, who rose to become that emperor's favorite until he was, with his master's approval, virtually wielding the imperial scepter himself, and who then, in one of the most spectacular reversals of fortune on record, was plummeted into disgrace and death in the space of a single day, and by the same Tiberius to whom he owed his vertiginous rise. In Tacitus, however, Sejanus' career forms only an epicycle in a larger pattern, the process whereby Rome lost its freedom and deteriorated, under Tiberius, into an odious tyranny.

Jonson adopts much of Tacitus' ethical pattern and something of Tacitus' bleak and forbidding tone as well. The fact that Sejanus has been destroyed by the end of the play is not permitted to afford us much satisfaction or much hope for the future. Behind the figure of the dead Sejanus looms the grimmer figure of Tiberius, still very much alive, while in the foreground looms the sinister shape of a new henchman, Sertorius Macro. We have no reason to doubt the accuracy of Arruntius' prediction that Macro will prove a worse scourge to Rome than Sejanus. Most of the men of good will have been liquidated in the course of the action, and neither the cowardly Senate nor the hysterical populace offer any rational ground for hope. Readers of Tacitus would remember that Sejanus' downfall in fact initiated an epoch of much more savage repression, in which Tiberius cast aside all restraint and turned himself into something like the systematic persecutor of his subjects.

Critics have noticed that Jonson, in composing dramatic characters from historical persons, seems deliberately to sidestep opportunities for complexity. His characters display a stubborn fixedness, a refusal to change or grow, an absence of introspection, reminiscent of their author's comic creations. Jonson achieves this simplicity in a variety of ways. Sometimes he suppresses mention of inconsistent traits, or remains silent about conflicting bits of information; sometimes he preserves minor inconsistencies, but manages to keep them peripheral and subordinate. One favorite technique is to incorporate refractory detail in a context that effectively neutralizes it. Thus disparagement of Agrippina is placed in the mouth of Sejanus, where it seems like praise, and Silius' boasts concerning his service to the state are made one item in the bill of complaints hurled at him by the repellent public prosecutor, Afer, so that we are inclined to discount them, if not disbelieve them.

If we ask why Jonson should thus have simplified, thus expressly declined the possibilities of psychological complexity in his characters, we may guess, at a venture, that he wished to avoid, precisely, the mixed and contradictory effect that Sidney had singled out as a defect in the real persons of history. Jonson aims at exemplary characters, from whom audiences may take their own moral bearings. He also aims at a certain clarity of effect, wherein oppositions between good and evil register sharply. The result, we may add, is never copybook stereotype or a facile retreat into abstraction, but magnification of those traits chosen for emphasis. By doing away with petty inconsistencies in his characters, Jonson does away with pettiness; he achieves the "dignity of persons" he proposed to himself as one prime requisite of tragic art.

In Sejanus, Jonson constructs a character who could hardly have been predicted from the annals. Confronted with Sejanus' prodigious successes, and with the rather ordinary figure he cuts otherwise, Jonson has chosen to model him on a stage type. He accounts for his triumphs by giving him the attributes of the Senecan villain, the ambitious titan who glories in his own criminality and makes of it the measure of his superiority to other men. He accounts for the impermanence of those triumphs by positing, along with the titanism and the appetite for evil, a fatal obtuseness that makes of Sejanus, finally, only a pawn in the hands of his immensely more cunning master.

The theatrical context is in fact essential to Jonson's view of history: he sees men as types, as *characters*, as actors on the great stage of time, and he takes pains to make them both consistent and convincing in their roles. Tiberius was needed for the role of the tyrant, and in his historical self he fitted almost perfectly— but not quite. The historians report various discrepancies between the younger Tiberius and the older, as well as between the early and later years of his reign. As a young man Tiberius showed not only military and executive talent but humanity in his dealings with others. His loyalty to his first wife; his apparent indifference to power, suggested by the retirement to Rhodes at a moment when to retire meant to forfeit the good graces of Augustus and seriously impair his own chances for the succession; his helpful, tactful conduct while on Rhodes; and the modesty with which he at first bore himself as emperor—all this implies a character more various in his possibilities than the monster of the final years. Suetonius and Tacitus, "bound to tell things as things were," report the early good behavior, viewing it, on the whole, as a mere semblance of virtue, a series of feints whereby Tiberius tried to divert attention from his vices, and which he gradually discarded until, at length, he revealed himself openly to be what he had always been in secret, a sadist and a degenerate. Jonson, utilizing his prerogative as poet, omits all reference to an earlier Tiberius. We see him in the play only as he is at the moment of the action, so sunk in duplicity as to be incapable of a candid word, and wholly devoted to the pursuit of his private obscenities. On the other hand, Jonson's Tiberius never impresses us, as the figure in the chronicles sometimes does, as a near psychotic, living in fright and disarray, paralyzed by superstition, and in spirit as tormented as the most abject of his victims, because this

too would interfere with the Jonsonian moral. What we do see is
a Tiberius monolithically dedicated to evil, who demonstrates,
in all his actions, "nothing that is not to be shunned."

It is with the good characters, however, that Jonson seems
most plainly to be pursuing a formula akin to Sidney's, scouring
from his historical originals the specks of vice or meanness that
blemish them as patterns of virtue. Critics who tax Jonson with
painting an unnaturally black world have done little justice to
his treatment of nearly the whole Germanican party, on whose
members he confers a dignity and a moral authority that they
were in fact far from possessing. Tacitus describes the historical
Agrippina as querulous and insubordinate, suspicious and
recriminatory. The incitements of Sejanus' agents were scarcely
needed to goad her into outbreaks of resentment: by her
restlessness she played into his hands. Jonson has preserved this
aspect of her only in some uncomplimentary remarks of Sejanus,
where we tend to disallow them, and in her generally forthright
manner. But he has given her a significant speech on stoic
patience that her turbulent original would never have uttered,
and, more important, he has fostered the impression, which
Tacitus does not, that she and her house constituted a moral as
well as a geographical rallying point for the followers of her dead
husband.

In the first act of the play Drusus Senior, the son of Tiberius,
becomes a hero briefly, by striking Sejanus in public, whereupon
the crowd acclaims him "a Castor." The nickname "Castor,"
taken from a celebrated gladiator of the day, had indeed been
conferred on the historical Drusus, but in a less complimentary
spirit—because of his violent temper and his notorious fondness
for blood. Drusus was cruel, so cruel, says Dio, that the sharpest
swords were called Drusian after him.[4] Suetonius describes him

---

4. *Dio's Roman History* 57.14.9–10, trans. Earnest Cary, Loeb Classics, 7
(London, 1924), 148–49.

as vicious and dissolute in his habits.[5] But when Arruntius, in the first scene of the play, speaks slightingly of him as "a riotous youth," his companions counter with a panegyric of his generosity and mettle. Nothing, finally, in the play suggests that Drusus is other than a rugged, admirable patriot who refuses to knuckle under to his father's detested favorite. Jonsonian tragedy would seem to decree that Sejanus' enemies must not be tainted with Sejanus' faults.

Nor must Sejanus' enemies be linked, if avoidable, with his allies. Jonson maintains silence on the fact that Livia, wife to Drusus and mistress of Sejanus, who intrigues with her lover to murder her husband, was also the sister of Germanicus. By ignoring this fact, Jonson seems to be ruling out what he may have felt as an embarrassing complication, the collusion of Germanicus' own sister in the ruin of her brother's house.

Caius Silius, the renowned general who becomes Sejanus' first victim in the campaign against the Germanicans, provides a good illustration of the sort of historical personage Sidney found defective. Tacitus never questions Silius' soldiership, or his administrative competence, or the unjust manner of his trial. He does, however, make it clear that Silius and his wife, during their years in the provinces, were guilty of extortion as charged, and that Silius had certainly boasted recklessly of the loyalty of his troops, and of the debt the emperor owed him. By failing even to hint that the extortion charge might be true, by having Silius ringingly brand it a lie, Jonson himself converts it into a falsehood, and by placing the charge of boasting in the mouth of Afer, he makes it seem like the spiteful exaggeration of a professional informer. Moreover, by giving Silius the great speech in which he turns the accusation against his accusers, by having him consciously set his friends an example of stoic fortitude,

---

5. Suetonius, *Tiberius* 52, in *Works*, trans. J. C. Rolfe, Loeb Classics, 1 (London, 1914), 364–65.

Jonson makes him heroic. He transforms him from an unsatisfactory, because imperfect and contradictory, human being into
a "perfect pattern."

In the case of Titius Sabinus, Jonson has sifted out not crime
but weakness. As Tacitus reports it, Sabinus fell into the trap
set by Latiaris and the rest because, after years of frustrating
silence, he was eager to spill his grievances. As soon as Latiaris
struck the right note of sympathetic concern, Sabinus "burst
into tearful complaint."[6] Thereafter he did so on many occasions,
seeking out Latiaris in order to dilate on his distresses. Sabinus
in the play, by contrast, is a figure of commanding presence, who
speaks ill of Tiberius only after prodding, and then only with
stern reminders to Latiaris of the dangers of self-pity, and with a
strict refusal to entertain thoughts of sedition. By eliminating,
also, the scene in Tacitus in which Sabinus, having been accused
before the Senate, is dragged away, "crying (as loudly as the
cloak muffling his mouth and the noose round his neck allowed)
that this was a fine New Year ceremony—this year's sacrifice
was to Sejanus" (p. 187), Jonson omits an episode which is not
merely horrible but grotesque. It has a touch of buffoonery
about it; it degrades Sabinus by putting him too vividly in the
posture of the victim, and so impairs his moral dignity. By
transposing the episode into the more intimate setting of a
private house, Jonson allows Sabinus to preserve a visible and
manifest superiority to his assailants, even as they drag him away.

Of Marcus Lepidus, the worthy old senator who acts as one
spokesman for the party of virtue, Tacitus tells us that throughout
the worst of the Tiberian terror he retained the favor of the
emperor, and was able to play a wise and moderating role in

---

6. *Annals of Imperial Rome*, trans. Michael Grant, Penguin Classics (rev.
ed. London, 1959), p. 186. Parenthetical page numbers after quotations
from Tacitus will refer to this edition. See also the Notes following
the text.

events. Jonson, seeking to deepen the gulf between the innocent
and the guilty, implies, if he does not openly state, that Lepidus
is an enemy to Tiberius. By keeping silent on the subject of the
emperor's favor, Jonson removes the element of anomaly which
even Tacitus finds puzzling in the spectacle of a good man being
approved by a wicked ruler.[7] As for Lucius Arruntius, Tacitus
does speak of him as "immaculate" (p. 197), but keeps him
a supernumerary, a figure half-glimpsed in a crowded pageant,
whereas Jonson brings him into the foreground and assigns him
a key position as observer and commentator. He makes Arruntius
not so much an object of emulation as the conscience of the play,
the virtuous onlooker who registers most sharply, if sometimes
with bewilderment, the impact of events, and through whose
indignant reactions our own are filtered.

Probably only two characters can be said to preserve intact
the inconsistencies of their Tacitean originals, but for special
reasons. One, Asinius Gallus, represents the Character of a
Trimmer: he flatters the emperor, but secretly favors the
opposition, and illustrates the futility of trying to appease a
tyrant. The other, Terentius, follows Sejanus, but more from
personal loyalty than opportunism. He thus maintains a claim

---

7. Even so, Jonson does not wholly avoid making Lepidus appear a time-
server. In his one senatorial act in the play, directly after the suicide of
Silius, Lepidus argues humanely that the Treasury should confiscate only
a fourth of Silius' estate, rather than the half proposed by Gallus:

> . . . the rest go to the children;
> Wherein the prince shall show humanity
> And bounty, not to force them by their want—
> *Which in their parents' trespass they deserved—*
> To take ill courses. [III.361–5]

The italicized line (my italics) represents a major concession to evil: in
order to exercise his restraining effect, Lepidus is forced to concur in the
assumption that Silius and Sosia were guilty of treason, which we know
he knows to be a tyrant's falsehood.

on our respect, and earns the right to pronounce the final words on the villain, to ask pity for him and moralize on his downfall.

"Misery," says Tacitus, in connection with Sabinus, "is demoralizing" (p. 186). The terrible thing in Tacitus is to watch even the good men lose their equilibrium and self-respect. But in *Sejanus* the persecuted Germanicans are ennobled rather than degraded by suffering. Jonson endows them, furthermore, with a full awareness, such as their historical originals could scarcely have had, of their roles as champions of a vanishing liberty. In so doing he makes them worthy spokesmen for the ethical values he approves, and worthy antagonists, in moral stature if not in political effectiveness, for Tiberius and Sejanus.

The world of *Sejanus*, then, contains far more untarnished virtue than the imperial Rome of Tacitus. If the play's conclusion approaches Tacitus in its pessimism, it nevertheless leaves us with the reflection, more decisively than Tacitus, that during the worst visitations of tyranny there will always remain adherents to old-fashioned honor who cannot be terrorized. The victims of tyranny in Jonson, by refusing to be intimidated, maintain their moral identities intact; they show us "each thing to be followed," and so assist in that perfecting of our own moral instincts which Sidney regarded as the aim of literature. Jonsonian tragedy thus performs as clear a corrective purpose as Jonsonian comedy. Where the one attempts to laugh us out of our follies, the other attempts to fortify us in our virtues. The comedies enjoin us not to become the dupes of rogues and charlatans. The tragedies teach us to steel ourselves against disaster, and so defeat it.

*Sejanus*, however, is more than a play about ancient Rome: it glances at conditions in Jacobean England. For Jonson and his contemporaries, history had meaning largely for what it could teach about the present. *Sejanus*, acted in 1603, was so far from being a mere academic reconstruction of the past that it seems to have led to Jonson's being cited before the Privy Council on charges of treason. As to the exact charges, one can only speculate, but one may note that any play performed in 1603 which dealt with the downfall and execution of a powerful favorite, a favorite who aspired to unseat the monarch he served, that monarch, in turn, being notably vacillating and enigmatic in character—any such play would probably be taken as alluding, however distantly, to the career of the Earl of Essex, which had followed a roughly analogous course two years earlier, and was still one of the delicate issues of the day, "somewhat queasy to be touched." Perhaps more objectionable to the authorities was the depiction of a government tyranny establishing itself through the use of informers. Tacitus portrays, and Jonson re-creates with all the resources at his command, the spectacle of a whole nation turning into a race of spies and eavesdroppers. A situation in which informers were encouraged to bring charges in hopes of inheriting the property of their victims, in which innocent remarks, half-remarks, and non-remarks were made pretexts for accusations of treason, in which informers enjoyed the protection of the law, but not their victims—such a situation was not without its parallels in England in Jonson's day, especially in the Roman Catholic circles to which Jonson at this time belonged, and against which the government was proceeding somewhat as Tiberius proceeded against the Germanicans.

We may point to the indictment of Cremutius Cordus in Act III as the disclaimer of relevance that paradoxically clinches the relevance. Cordus' own annals (surviving only in fragments), we may assume, were what they purported to be—a record of the past, innocent of allusion to the present. Nor need we doubt that Tacitus, in putting into Cordus' mouth an impassioned defense of the historian's freedom of subject, was genuinely indignant at the practice of reading topical meanings into historical texts.

But Jonson's use of that same oration (translated whole out of
Tacitus, as he told Drummond) is another matter. Jonson had
always been haunted by the specter of spies and state agents. On
more than one occasion he had suffered from their zeal.[8] In
prologue, epigram, and dramatic fable he had denounced—and
would again denounce—the breed of troublemakers who
attended plays mainly to discover seditious implications in them,
and who, when they could not find them, would invent them
by alleging double meanings and concealed identities. He
reserved his sharpest scorn, in *Poetaster*, for the officious tribune
Lupus, zealous in the discovery of nonexistent conspiracies and
incriminating emblems. The choice of the Tiberian court as a
setting for *Sejanus*, the working up of a thick atmosphere of
delation and cloaked collusion, testify to Jonson's desire to
expose anew the old unwholesome state of mind. By making
Cordus attack the abusive reading of historical books, Jonson is
once again challenging the practice he has criticized so often.
Only he is making history do just what his own historian,
Cordus, claims it does not do—reflect on the present times. No
doubt Sejanus' onslaught on Cordus takes its place as one item
more in the repressive mechanisms of the police state, proceeding
by willful misconstruction of evidence to stamp out independent
thought. The weakness in Cordus' defense lies in its element of
disingenuousness, in Jonson's reluctance to admit that historical

---

8. As in 1597, when he was imprisoned for his share in the lost comedy
of *The Isle of Dogs*, which had been denounced to the Privy Council as a
"lewd plaie," containing "very seditious & sclandrous matter" (Herford
and Simpson, *Ben Jonson*, 1, 217–18). As also in 1598, when he was,
according to his account to Drummond, set upon during a second im-
prisonment by "two damn'd Villans to catch advantage of him" (*Conversations with Drummond of Hawthornden*, 256–60), apparently to draw him
into treasonable remarks as a consequence of his recent conversion to
Roman Catholicism.

writing does, sometimes, allude to current events and is designed to illuminate them. We have, then, the odd spectacle of a manifesto of the disinterestedness of historical writing in a piece of historical writing that is itself anything but disinterested

Jonson would not, of course, have wished his auditors to think that his play was antiseptically sterile of reference to immediate political realities, but simply that it contained no specific allusions to particular persons or events. So much, judging from the text as we have it, may well have been true. On the premise that human nature does not vary much from age to age, he aimed to exhibit the behavior of *homo politicus* in all ages. He showed ancient Romans trapped in a desperate situation partly visited on them, partly of their own making, so as to serve warning on his fellow citizens of the risks they were running by yielding to the conspiratorial mentality. On this point the timeliness of the play has hardly diminished with the passage of centuries. When Hazlitt set out to anthologize his favorite scenes, he confessed himself "half afraid" to give his extracts,

> lest they should be tortured into an application to other times and characters than those referred to by the poet. Some of the sounds, indeed, may bear (for what I know) an awkward construction: some of the objects may look double to squint-eyed suspicion. But that is not my fault. It only proves, that the characters of prophet and poet are implied in each other; that he who describes human nature well once, describes it for good and all, as it was, is, and, I begin to fear, will ever be. Truth always was, and must always remain a libel to the tyrant and the slave.[9]

Governments have not grown notably less suspicious than Tacitus' Rome, or Jonson's or Hazlitt's England, nor have zealots flagged in their self-appointed spying and denouncing. That Jonson could not frankly acknowledge the tendentiousness of his

9. William Hazlitt, *Lectures on the Dramatic Literature of the Age of Elizabeth* (3d ed. London, 1840), pp. 155–56.

play testifies more than anything else to the curbs placed on free expression by fearful despots. Had the time been free, had the age been good, *Sejanus* would not have had to be written at all. Even with its component of compromise, it remains one of the most devastating accounts the drama has given us of dictatorship in action.

*Sejanus*, then, dramatizes the decline of Roman liberty, and warns Englishmen against allowing it to happen to them. It presents a series of exemplary figures from whose fate spectators may learn moral courage, and perhaps acquire some rules of thumb for survival. In it history is transmuted into both poetry and political discourse. Is it also tragedy? Jonson himself, in his address to the reader, enumerates four requirements of tragedy he believes he has met: "Truth of argument, dignity of persons, gravity and height of elocution, fullness and frequency of sentence"—or, in other words, historical accuracy, grandeur of characters, rhetorical elevation, and weight and abundance of moral reflections. As commentators have noticed, all but one of these (and that one in part) concern the play as rhetoric rather than as action. Jonson's tragedies notoriously refuse to conform to Aristotelian canons. One critic, noting that *Sejanus* contains no tragic hero, sees it as "concerned with the tragic flaw *within the social order*, not within the individual," with "the manner in which evil penetrates the political structure."[10] Another, again usefully, proposes to classify the play, along with *Catiline*, as "Renaissance tragedy," to distinguish it from both classic and Elizabethan versions of the genre.[11]

Such redefinition and reclassification, while it helps us see the

10. K. M. Burton, "The Political Tragedies of Chapman and Ben Jonson," *Essays in Criticism*, 2 (1952), 397, 404.

11. Ralph Nash, "Jonson's Tragic Poems," *Studies in Philology*, 55 (1958), 185.

play in its proper light, is unlikely to persuade readers that it produces a "tragic effect," and we might once more ask why this should be so. Why, given the gravity of the subject and all that Jonson has done to vitalize it, should it not stir "tragic" emotion? Partly, no doubt, because it *is* "Renaissance" tragedy, because Jonson hews closely to the public aspects of his story, and treats those aspects as occasions for rhetorical debate rather than lyric effusion. Jonson avoids the effects of pathos and "private" feeling that often add resonance to the harshness of tragic disasters. He shows us only the patriotic indignation of his good characters, not their domestic misfortunes, and he confines our view of the evil characters to their deeds of malice. When Jonson's villains soliloquize, they measure out for us the full length and breadth of their villainy, but they disclose no uncertainty, no flickers of self-doubt to contradict their decisions. Their errors, as one critic has said, "are at bottom mathematical, and they fail because their calculations are inaccurate."[12]

We feel a slight constriction in the presence of these soliloquizing villains; we feel that they know more about themselves than they are telling us, that they are not really soliloquizing. And this feeling spreads to our sense of the evil in the play as a whole: Jonson blocks access to any account of it that might resist rational explanation. Tragedy characteristically allows the evil it portrays to remain to some degree inexplicable. It shows the gap between human intentions and human acts, or between acts and their consequences. It shows the most intensely ideated human plans wrecked by factors beyond human control. Forces variously conceived as chance, fate, fortune, necessity, or God reach down and trouble the current of human affairs. Yet Jonson comes close to fixing exact and entire responsibility on human agency. In *Sejanus* the margin allowed to unseen or unknown

---

12. W. D. Briggs, ed., *Sejanus* (Boston, 1911), p. xxxii.

or uncontrollable forces dwindles nearly to the vanishing point. Our lives, Jonson wishes to declare, are in our own power.

As the play opens, the virtuous Germanicans are discussing the state of servitude into which Rome is falling. In the manly accents that Jonson gives them, they accept responsibility for the situation. "All is worthy of us, were it more," affirms Silius, "Who with our riots, pride, and civil hate, / Have so provoked the justice of the gods." To Sabinus' observation that the times have deteriorated since the great days of Caesar and Pompey, Arruntius replies with an impassioned indictment of "the men." "The men are not the same! 'Tis we are base, / Poor, and degenerate from th'exalted strain / Of our great fathers." He cites Cato, Brutus, and Cassius as "mighty spirits" whose fire has gone out in men's bosoms. A moment later the theme of the dead hero is resumed, *fortissimo*, in the eulogy of Germanicus, who is said to have combined in himself the great qualities of all the others.

We may notice in this, first, Jonson's care to make guilt a collective matter. He will not allow us to foist responsibility for evil onto the shoulders of a few criminals. If ill prevails, it is because good men have insufficiently combated it. At the same time, we must see that this doctrine is inadequate to explain the evil in this world. Germanicus, with all his nobility, fell victim to Tiberius as unresistingly as any character in the play, yet there is no suggestion that he should or could have acted otherwise than he did. His very innocence was part of his nobility. Nor do we find it easy to imagine others, placed in the situations of Silius, Sabinus, Lepidus, and Arruntius, acquitting themselves more honorably or opposing evil more effectively. If the men are base, poor, and degenerate from what they were, we want to know why. If "heaven's anger against Rome" accounts here, as in Tacitus (p. 153), for Sejanus' ascendancy, we would like to ask: Why should heaven *be* angry with Rome?—angrier, that is, than at any other time?

Introduction

Jonson, to get at the matter in another way, attempts to present a world totally explicable in rational terms. Good and evil appear more as intellectual preferences than as irrational instincts. Tiberius and Sejanus, we feel, have chosen their present course of action deliberately. They have adopted it as an operational procedure, and pursue it in full consciousness of cause. Few of the characters act from impulse or forgetfulness, or in a manner inconsistent with their conscious goals. When logical explanations reach their limit, Jonson will have no recourse to illogical ones. Though he speaks of the gods, he does not make us feel them lurking at the fringes of the action. He avoids creating the aura of wonder that tinges the woe in so much other tragedy. If the portents in Act V lack resonance compared to their counterparts in *Julius Caesar*, it is because one feels that Jonson does not believe in them any more than Sejanus does. He uses them as a way of displaying Sejanus' hubris, but he does not imply that the disbelief in them betrays a defect of Sejanus' imagination, nor that by defying them Sejanus is disturbing any watchful presences. Terentius' piety, the invocations to the gods frequent among the good characters, seem designed chiefly to exhibit the loyalty of these characters to traditional sanctities, rather than to express a felt sense of the presence of surveillant powers. On the other hand, Marcus Lepidus certainly speaks for his creator when he declares (V.733–34) that Fortune would have no deity if men had wisdom. Fortune, at base, is a metaphor, a desperate trope whereby men shirk the consequences of their own folly.

The result is that when we try to locate the source of evil in the play, we find ourselves balked. "*Sejanus*," correctly observes a recent critic, "implies that the ultimate reality of politics is the amoral struggle for power in which the fittest survive."[13] But

---

13. Robert Ornstein, *The Moral Vision of Jacobean Tragedy* (Madison, Wisc., 1960), p. 88.

behind the struggle, what? Only a species of cosmic luck, never acknowledged as such; the personality of the ruler takes on the attributes of fate. In *Catiline*, only the fact that a patriot, Cicero, is at the helm permits Catiline's conspiracy to be uprooted; otherwise we find ourselves among men (and women) much like those in *Sejanus*. Only the fact that *Poetaster* is set in the reign of Augustus permits it to be a comedy, permits the vicious, meddlesome tribune Lupus and his scurrilous associates to be defeated, first by judgment, then by laughter. And only the fact that it is Tiberius who rules the world of *Sejanus* enforces on events in that play their appalling course. The cruelty and dishonesty that Cicero succeeds in controlling, that Augustus can curb and turn to a joke, are licensed, are unleashed and given countenance, in *Sejanus*, by the grim figure of Tiberius.

Yet Jonson does not encourage us to see matters in such a light. His play, with its incisive depiction of evil, blocks our deepest understanding of that evil by lodging it too strictly in the ethical realm, and his efforts to ascribe the temporary setback of evil to the gods suffers from the evident fact that the gods have nothing to do with it. Though Arruntius moralizes on "slippery chance," chance is rigorously excluded from any partnership in events. No coincidences worth mentioning occur, nor can anything in the action be termed accidental except the collapse of the grotto, which merely delays, without altering, the outcome. The one purely fortuitous stage encounter, that between Sejanus and Drusus at the end of Act I, produces a vivid theatrical clash that is, immediately afterward, expressly declared *not* to have affected the inexorable march of events. *Sejanus*, in one respect, conforms all too completely to Aristotle, to the dictum that tragical episodes should arise from each other by necessity or probability. By contriving to make all episodes arise so, Jonson forbids the random combinations, the unpredictable conjunctions—the operation, in short, of extrahuman factors which, we feel, enter into and decisively affect the texture of existence.

Jonson, we might say, has constructed his tragic plot with something of the strict logicality he brings to comic plotting. Comedy invites us to see human beings as overdetermined, as conforming too severely to the self-imposed laws of their own existence. Tragedy might perhaps invite us to lament these same rigidities, but in fact, *Sejanus* tries to argue us simultaneously into a belief that we are free, which we see to be not the case, and that the gods are near, which we see equally to be not the case. Jonson's personages believe themselves free, act as though free, accept responsibility for their acts, yet all the while are being ground to pieces in an engine not of their own making.

So much may help us understand why, despite the play's evident grandeur, it does not have certain effects commonly demanded of tragedy. It is great in its own way and on its own terms. Power, intensity, and articulate design lie before us in profusion. *Sejanus* deals with evil on a monumental scale and with happenings of unarguable significance. It engages us from the outset with the precision and live force of its language: everything that happens happens in a context of intense moral discrimination, and Jonson's rhetoric is equal to all its occasions. The huge crises, when they come, have the jolting impact of geological cataclysms, the product of centuries of shifting of subterranean rock. They may not console us, but they are not meant to. They confront us with the facts of our nature and the evil in our lives, and suggest the kinds of strength we may summon from ourselves to meet the evil. *Sejanus* faces, as tragedy must, the worst potentialities of human nature, and by realizing them dramatically, acts to inhibit their further actualization in reality. It exploits the evil in the world so as to promote the good in its audiences.

# TO THE NO LESS
# NOBLE, BY VIRTUE
# THAN BLOOD:
[5]         # ESME, LORD AUBIGNY

MY LORD,                                                            5

If ever any ruin were so great as to survive, I think this be one
I send you: *The Fall of Sejanus*. It is a poem that—if I well
remember—in your Lordship's sight, suffered no less violence
[10] from our people here than the subject of it did from the rage of
the people of Rome, but with a different fate, as (I hope) merit.    10
For this hath outlived their malice, and begot itself a greater
favor than he lost, the love of good men. Amongst whom, if I
[15] make your Lordship the first it thanks, it is not without a just
confession of the bond your benefits have, and ever shall hold
upon me.                                                           15

                           Your Lordship's most faithful honorer,
                                         *Ben. Jonson.*

4 ESME, LORD AUBIGNY N. (*N. refers throughout to corresponding note at end of
text.*) *The bracketed line references accompanying the Dedication, the
Address to the Readers, the Argument, and Tiberius' letter to the Senate
(V.546–658 below) will be to Herford and Simpson's edition of the play
(4, 349–470): but the notes, glossarial and otherwise, to the same portions
of the play, except for V.546–658, will be to the line numbers of the present
edition, indicated in the usual manner without brackets.*

6 RUIN *Jonson seems to be thinking of an architectural ruin which survives the
defacements of vandals. See III.749.*

8 IN . . . SIGHT *Aubigny having been present at the disastrous first Globe
performance.*

8–9 SUFFERED . . . HERE *Sejanus was badly received, evidently because of its
lengthy speeches and paucity of spectacle.*

11–12 BEGOT . . . MEN *referring to the commendatory verses prefixed to the 1605
Quarto, in which Jonson's friends expressed their indignation at the
play's failure.*

## To the Readers

The following and voluntary labors of my friends, prefixed to my book, have relieved me in much, whereat (without them) I should necessarily have touched. Now I will only use three or four short and needful notes, and so rest. [5]

5    First, if it be objected that what I publish is no true poem in the strict laws of time, I confess it; as also in the want of a proper chorus, whose habit and moods are such and so difficult as not any whom I have seen since the ancients—no, not they who have most presently affected laws—have yet come in the way of. Nor [10]

10   is it needful, or almost possible, in these our times, and to such auditors as commonly things are presented, to observe the old state and splendor of dramatic poems, with preservation of any popular delight. But of this I shall take more seasonable cause to [15] speak, in my observations upon Horace his *Art of Poetry* which,

1–2 THE FOLLOWING . . . BOOK *the laudatory verses from friends included as prefatory matter to the Quarto.*

2–3 HAVE . . . TOUCHED *have made it needless for me to mention many things I would otherwise have had to discuss.*

5–6 NO TRUE . . . TIME N.

5 POEM *dramatic poem, tragedy.*

6–7 PROPER CHORUS *i.e. after the manner of classic drama. In his next tragedy, Catiline, Jonson did introduce a formal chorus.*

9 PRESENTLY *lately.* AFFECTED LAWS *insisted on the "rules" of dramatic composition.* N.

9–13 NOR IS . . . DELIGHT N.

13 SEASONABLE CAUSE *appropriate occasion.*

14 OBSERVATIONS . . . POETRY *written but never published, and later destroyed by the fire in Jonson's library in 1623.*

with the text translated, I intend shortly to publish. In the mean- <sup>15</sup>
time, if in truth of argument, dignity of persons, gravity and
height of elocution, fullness and frequency of sentence, I have
[20] discharged the other offices of a tragic writer, let not the absence
of these forms be imputed to me, wherein I shall give you
occasion hereafter (and without my boast) to think I could better    20
prescribe, than omit the due use for want of a convenient
[25] knowledge.

The next is, lest in some nice nostril the quotations might
savor affected, I do let you know that I abhor nothing more;
and have only done it to show my integrity in the story, and    25
save myself in those common torturers that bring all wit to the
[30] rack; whose noses are ever like swine spoiling and rooting up
the muses' gardens, and their whole bodies, like moles, as
blindly working under earth to cast any—the least—hills upon
virtue.    30

Whereas they are in Latin, and the work in English, it was
[35] presupposed none but the learned would take the pains to confer
them, the authors themselves being all in the learned tongues
save one, with whose English side I have had little to do: to
which it may be required, since I have quoted the page, to name    35

---

16 TRUTH OF ARGUMENT *fidelity to history.* N. PERSONS *characters.*

17 SENTENCE *aphorism, or moral maxim, as found in classical tragedy, especially
Seneca.*

23 NICE *fastidious.* QUOTATIONS *the marginal notes to the 1605 Quarto, in
which Jonson cites his sources.*

24 SAVOR AFFECTED *smack of affectation.*

25 INTEGRITY . . . STORY *faithfulness to history.*

26 IN *from.* WIT *intellectual endeavor.*

27 SPOILING *destroying.*

31 THEY *the historical sources.*

32 CONFER *compare.*

34 ONE *Tacitus, translated in 1598 by Richard Greneway.*

what edition I followed. *Tacit. Lips.* in 4°. *Antwerp. edit* 1600. *Dio. Folio Hen. Step.* 92. For the rest, as *Sueton. Seneca.* etc., the [40] chapter doth sufficiently direct, or the edition is not varied.

40 Lastly, I would inform you that this book, in all numbers, is not the same with that which was acted on the public stage, wherein a second pen had good share; in place of which I have [45] rather chosen to put weaker (and no doubt less pleasing) of mine own, than to defraud so happy a genius of his right by my loathed usurpation.

45 Fare you well, and if you read farther of me, and like, I shall not be afraid of it, though you praise me out. [50]

*Neque enim mihi cornea fibra est.*

But that I should plant my felicity in your general saying "Good," or "Well," etc., were a weakness which the better sort
50 of you might worthily contemn, if not absolutely hate me for. [55]

BEN. JONSON. and no such,
*Quem Palma negata macrum, donata reducit opimum.*

39 NUMBERS *verses.*
41 SECOND PEN *N.*
46 OUT *thoroughly.*
47 NEQUE . . . EST *"For my fibre is not of horn"* (Persius, Satires, *1.47–8*). *I.e. I am not impervious to praise.*
52 QUEM . . . OPIMUM *"Whom the denial of the palm sends home lean, and the bestowal of it well-fed"* (Horace, Epistles, *2.1.181*). *I.e. whose happiness depends on the favorable reception of his play by the public.*

Aelius Sejanus, son to Sejus Strabo, a gentleman of Rome, and
born at Vulsinium, after his long service in court—first under
Augustus, afterward Tiberius—grew into that favor with the
latter, and won him by those arts, as there wanted nothing but
[5]   the name to make him a copartner of the empire. Which great-      5
ness of his, Drusus, the emperor's son, not brooking, after many
smothered dislikes, it one day breaking out, the prince struck
him publicly on the face. To revenge which disgrace, Livia,
the wife of Drusus (being before corrupted by him to her
[10]  dishonor, and the discovery of her husband's counsels) Sejanus   10
practiseth with, together with her physician, called Eudemus,
and one Lygdus, an eunuch, to poison Drusus. This their
inhuman act having successful and unsuspected passage, it
emboldeneth Sejanus to farther and more insolent projects,
[15]  even the ambition of the empire; where finding the lets he must   15
encounter to be many and hard, in respect of the issue of Germanicus (who were next in hope for the succession) he deviseth
to make Tiberius' self his means, and instills into his ears many
doubts and suspicions, both against the princes and their mother
[20]  Agrippina; which Caesar jealously hearkening to, as covetously   20

17 in hope . . . succession)] in hope) Q *N.*

---

9 BEFORE CORRUPTED *correct historically, but Jonson, in fact, makes the
corruption of Livia happen only* after *the blow on the face.*
11 PRACTISETH *conspires.*
13 SUCCESSFUL . . . PASSAGE *a successful outcome that arouses no suspicions.*
15 LETS *obstacles.*
20 JEALOUSLY *suspiciously.*

29

consenteth to their ruin, and their friends'. In this time, the better to mature and strengthen his design, Sejanus labors to marry Livia, and worketh, with all his engine, to remove Tiberius from the knowledge of public business, with allure-
25 ments of a quiet and retired life. The latter of which, Tiberius,   [25] out of a proneness to lust, and a desire to hide those unnatural pleasures which he could not so publicly practice, embraceth. The former enkindleth his fears, and there gives him first cause of doubt or suspect toward Sejanus; against whom he raiseth, in
30 private, a new instrument, one Sertorius Macro, and by him   [30] underworketh, discovers the other's counsels, his means, his ends; sounds the affections of the senators; divides, distracts them. At last, when Sejanus least looketh, and is most secure, with pretext of doing him an unwonted honor in the Senate he   [35]
35 trains him from his guards, and with a long doubtful letter, in one day hath him suspected, accused, condemned, and torn in pieces by the rage of the people.

22 Sejanus] he Q
25 retired] separated Q
35–36 guards . . . day] guards, with one letter, and in one day Q

23 ENGINE *strategy*.
31 UNDERWORKETH *tunnels from beneath*.
35 DOUBTFUL *ambiguous*.
37 THE PEOPLE *N*.

# The Persons of the Play

Tiberius, [Emperor of Rome]
Drusus Se[nior, his son]

Nero
Drusus Ju[nior]      } [sons of Agrippina]
[Caius] Caligula

[Lucius] Arruntius, [a senator]
[Caius] Silius, [a general]
[Titius] Sabinus, [a gentleman]    } [friends of Agrippina]
[Cremutius] Cordus, [a historian]
[Asinius] Gallus, [a senator]

[Marcus] Lepidus, [a senator]

[Lucius Aelius] Sejanus, [favorite of the emperor]

Eudemus, [a physician]
Terentius
Minutius           } [followers of Sejanus]
Satrius [Secundus]
[Pinnarius] Natta

Latiaris, [a senator]
Rufus              } [spies, friends of Sejanus]
Opsius

Cotta
[Quintus] Haterius
Sanquinius         } [senators, of Sejanus' faction]
Pomponius
[Julius] Posthumus

[Fulcinius] Trio, [consul, cohort of Sejanus]
[Memmius] Regulus, [consul]
Varro, [consul, cohort of Sejanus]

THE PERSONS OF THE PLAY N.

31

The Persons of the Play

[Gracinus] Laco, [commander of the night-watch]
[Sertorius] Macro, [prefect, creature of Tiberius]

Agrippina, [widow of Germanicus]
Livia, [wife to Drusus Senior]
Sosia, [wife to Caius Silius]

Flamen, [priest]
Servus, [slave]
Nuntius, [messenger]

Tribuni, [tribunes]
Lictores, [lictors]
Praecones, [heralds]
Tubicines, [trumpeters]
Tibicines, [flute-players]
Ministri, [assistants to the priest]

The Scene, *Rome*

# Act I

[*A state room in the palace. Enter*] *Sabinus* [*and*] *Silius,*
[*followed by Latiaris.*]

*Sabinus.* Hail, Caius Silius!
*Silius.*                  Titius Sabinus, hail!
You'are rarely met in court.
*Sabinus.*                 Therefore well met.
*Silius.* 'Tis true. Indeed, this place is not our sphere.
*Sabinus.* No, Silius, we are no good enginers.
We want the fine arts, and their thriving use          5
Should make us graced, or favored of the times.
We have no shift of faces, no cleft tongues,
No soft and glutinous bodies, that can stick
Like snails on painted walls; or, on our breasts
Creep up, to fall from that proud height to which     10
We did by slavery, not by service, climb.
We are no guilty men, and then no great.
We have nor place in court, office in state,
That we can say we owe unto our crimes.
We burn with no black secrets which can make      15

4 ENGINERS *plotters, intriguers.*
9 OR *i.e. nor can we.*
12 THEN *hence.*

33

Act I

Us dear to the authors, or live feared
Of their still waking jealousies, to raise
Ourselves a fortune by subverting theirs.
We stand not in the lines that do advance
To that so courted point.

[*Enter Satrius and Natta.*]

20      *Silius.*                    But yonder lean
A pair that do.
        *Sabinus.*        Good cousin Latiaris.
        *Silius.* Satrius Secundus and Pinnarius Natta,
The great Sejanus' clients. There be two,
Know more than honest counsels, whose close breasts
25    Were they ripped up to light, it would be found
A poor and idle sin, to which their trunks
Had not been made fit organs. These can lie,
Flatter, and swear, forswear, deprave, inform,
Smile, and betray; make guilty men; then beg
30    The forfeit lives, to get the livings; cut
Men's throats with whisp'rings; sell to gaping suitors
The empty smoke that flies about the palace;
Laugh when their patron laughs; sweat when he sweats;
Be hot and cold with him; change every mood,
35    Habit and garb, as often as he varies;
Observe him, as his watch observes his clock;

17 STILL . . . JEALOUSIES *perpetually active suspicions.*
19 IN THE LINES *i.e. along the road.*
20 LEAN *tend.*
24 CLOSE *secretive.*
26 TRUNKS *breasts.*
29 MAKE . . . MEN *make men guilty, by denouncing them to the authorities.*
29–30 BEG . . . LIVINGS *urge the death sentence, so that they will inherit the victims' property.*
36 OBSERVE *follow punctually.* HIS WATCH . . . CLOCK *N.*

And, true as turquoise in the dear lord's ring,
Look well or ill with him, ready to praise
His lordship if he spit, or but piss fair,
Have an indifferent stool, or break wind well—          40
Nothing can scape their catch.
   *Sabinus.*               Alas, these things
Deserve no note, conferred with other vile
And filthier flatteries that corrupt the times;
When not alone our gentry's chief are fain
To make their safety from such sordid acts,          45
But all our consuls, and no little part
Of such as have been praetors, yea, the most
Of senators, that else not use their voices,
Start up in public Senate, and there strive
Who shall propound most abject things, and base.          50
So much, as oft Tiberius hath been heard,
Leaving the court, to cry, "Oh race of men,
Prepared for servitude!" Which showed that he,
Who least the public liberty could like,
As loathly brooked their flat servility.          55
   *Silius.* Well, all is worthy of us, were it more,
Who with our riots, pride, and civil hate,
Have so provoked the justice of the gods—
We that within these fourscore years were born
Free, equal lords of the triumphèd world,          60
And knew no masters but affections;

37 TRUE . . . RING *Turquoise, sometimes worn in a ring as a charm, was thought to change color according to the mood of the wearer.*
41–55 N.
42 NOTE *notice.* CONFERRED *compared.*
48 SENATORS . . . VOICES N. ELSE *otherwise.*
56–74 N.
60 TRIUMPHÈD *conquered.*
61 AFFECTIONS *our own inclinations.*

To which betraying first our liberties,
We since became the slaves to one man's lusts,
And now to many. Every minist'ring spy
65  That will accuse and swear, is lord of you,
Of me, of all, our fortunes and our lives.
Our looks are called to question, and our words,
How innocent soever, are made crimes.
We shall not shortly dare to tell our dreams,
Or think, but 'twill be treason.
70      *Sabinus.*                    Tyrants' arts
Are to give flatterers grace, accusers power,
That those may seem to kill whom they devour.
                    [*Enter Cordus and Arruntius.*]
Now good Cremutius Cordus.
    *Cordus.*                    Hail to your lordship!
    *Natta.* Who's that salutes your cousin?          *They whisper.*
    *Latiaris.*                              'Tis one Cordus,
75  A gentleman of Rome, one that has writ
Annals of late, they say, and very well.
    *Natta.* Annals? Of what times?
    *Latiaris.*                    I think of Pompey's,
And Caius Caesar's, and so down to these.
    *Natta.* How stands h'affected to the present state?
80  Is he or Drusian, or Germanican?
Or ours, or neutral?
    *Latiaris.*          I know him not so far.
    *Natta.* Those times are somewhat queasy to be touched.
Have you or seen or heard part of his work?
    *Latiaris.* Not I; he means they shall be public shortly.

62 TO . . . LIBERTIES *sacrificing our freedom to the tyranny of our passions.*
64 MINIST'RING *obsequious.*
72 THOSE *flatterers and accusers.* THEY *tyrants.*
82 TOUCHED *referred to.*

*Natta.* Oh, Cordus do you call him?                              85

*Latiaris.*                                    Aye.

                              [*Exeunt Natta and Satrius.*]

*Sabinus.*                            But these our times

Are not the same, Arruntius.

    *Arruntius.*                          Times? The men,

The men are not the same! 'Tis we are base,

Poor, and degenerate from th'exalted strain

Of our great fathers. Where is now the soul

Of godlike Cato?—he that durst be good                          90

When Caesar durst be evil, and had power,

As not to live his slave, to die his master.

Or where the constant Brutus, that, being proof

Against all charm of benefits, did strike

So brave a blow into the monster's heart                        95

That sought unkindly to captive his country?

Oh, they are fled the light. Those mighty spirits

Lie raked up with their ashes in their urns,

And not a spark of their eternal fire

Glows in a present bosom. All's but blaze,                      100

Flashes, and smoke, wherewith we labor so.

There's nothing Roman in us, nothing good,

Gallant, or great. 'Tis true that Cordus says,

"Brave Cassius was the last of all that race."

---

90 CATO *Roman governor of Utica (95–46 B.C.), proverbial for his rectitude.*

91 WHEN . . . EVIL *N.*

92 AS . . . LIVE *by not living.*

93–4 PROOF . . . BENEFITS *immune to the corrupting effects of favors.*

96 UNKINDLY *unnaturally.* CAPTIVE *capture.*

100 A PRESENT BOSOM *the bosom of anyone alive.*

103 THAT *what.*

104 CASSIUS *Brutus' fellow-conspirator in the plot against Julius Caesar. See*
      *Shakespeare,* Julius Caesar, *V.3.99.*

*Sabinus.* Stand by! Lord Drusus.

                    *Drusus passeth by, [attended by Haterius.]*

105    *Haterius.*                Th'emp'ror's son! Give place!

    *Silius.* I like the prince well.

    *Arruntius.*           A riotous youth,

There's little hope of him.

    *Sabinus.*           That fault his age

Will, as it grows, correct. Methinks he bears

Himself each day more nobly than other,

110   And wins no less on men's affections

Than doth his father lose. Believe me, 'I love him,

And chiefly for opposing to Sejanus.

    *Silius.* And I for gracing his young kinsmen so,

The sons of Prince Germanicus. It shows

115  A gallant clearness in him, a straight mind,

That envies not, in them, their father's name.

    *Arruntius.* His name was, while he lived, above all envy;

And, being dead, without it. Oh, that man!

If there were seeds of the old virtue left,

They lived in him.

120  *Silius.*          He had the fruits, Arruntius,

More than the seeds. Sabinus and myself

Had means to know'him within, and can report him.

We were his followers, he would call us friends.

He was a man most like to virtue, 'in all

125  And every action, nearer to the gods

Than men in nature, of a body'as fair

---

113 kinsmen] kinsman Q

---

109 NOBLY *trisyllabic.* OTHER *i.e. the day before.*

115 CLEARNESS *nobility.*

118 IT *envy.*

122 WITHIN *intimately.*

As was his mind, and no less reverend
In face than fame. He could so use his state,
Temp'ring his greatness with his gravity,
As it avoided all self-love in him,                          130
And spite in others. What his funerals lacked
In images and pomp, they had supplied
With honorable sorrow, soldiers' sadness,
A kind of silent mourning, such as men
Who know no tears but from their captives, use            135
To show in so great losses.
   *Cordus.*               I thought once,
Considering their forms, age, manner of deaths,
The nearness of the places where they fell,
T'have paralleled him with great Alexander.
For both were of best feature, of high race,               140
Yeared but to thirty, and in foreign lands,
By their own people, alike made away.
   *Sabinus.* I know not, for his death, how you might wrest it,
But for his life, it did as much disdain
Comparison with that voluptuous, rash,                     145
Giddy, and drunken Macedon's, as mine
Doth with my bondman's. All the good in him,
His valor and his fortune, he made his.
But he had other touches of late Romans,
That more did speak him: Pompey's dignity,                 150

128 STATE *rank, station.*
128–54 N.
132 IMAGES AND POMP N.
135 KNOW . . . CAPTIVES *i.e. who have only seen other men, and those captives,*
    *weep.*
139 PARALLELED HIM N.
143 WREST IT *force a comparison.*
143–7 N.
150 SPEAK HIM *proclaim his qualities.*

## Act I

The innocence of Cato, Caesar's spirit,
Wise Brutus' temperance; and every virtue
Which, parted unto others, gave them name,
Flowed mixed in him. He was the soul of goodness,
155 And all our praises of him are like streams
Drawn from a spring, that still rise full and leave
The part remaining greatest.
    *Arruntius.*                I am sure
He was too great for us, and that they knew
Who did remove him hence.
    *Sabinus.*                 When men grow fast
160 Honored and loved, there is a trick in state,
Which jealous princes never fail to use,
How to decline that growth with fair pretext
And honorable colors of employment,
Either by embassy, the war, or such,
165 To shift them forth into another air,
Where they may purge, and lessen. So was he;
And had his seconds there, sent by Tiberius,
And his more subtle dam, to discontent him,
To breed and cherish mutinies, detract
170 His greatest actions, give audacious check

153 PARTED *distributed separately.* NAME *reputation.*
154 MIXED *mingled.*
156 STILL *always.*
159 FAST *firmly.*
162 DECLINE *repress.*
163 COLORS *outward tokens, appearances.*
165 SHIFT . . . AIR *transfer them to another (distant) territory.*
166 PURGE, AND LESSEN *i.e. be rendered harmless as rivals.*
167 SECONDS *followers.*
168 DAM *Tiberius' mother, Livia, second wife of the emperor Augustus, notorious for her wiliness.* DISCONTENT *vex.*
169 DETRACT *belittle.*

To his commands, and work to put him out
In open act of treason. All which snares
When his wise cares prevented, a fine poison
Was thought on, to mature their practices.

    *Sejanus, Terentius, Satrius, Natta, etc., pass over the stage.*

    *Cordus.* Here comes Sejanus.

    *Silius.*               Now observe the stoops,      175
The bendings, and the falls.

    *Arruntius.*           Most creeping base!

    *Sejanus.* [*To Natta.*] I note 'em well. No more. Say you?

    *Satrius.*                     My lord,
There is a gentleman of Rome would buy—

    *Sejanus.* How call you him you talked with?

    *Satrius.*                 Please your lordship,
It is Eudemus, the physician                        180
To Livia, Drusus' wife.

    *Sejanus.*       On with your suit.
Would buy, you said—

    *Satrius.*         A tribune's place, my lord.

    *Sejanus.* What will he give?

    *Satrius.*           Fifty sestertia.

    *Sejanus.* Livia's physician, say you, is that fellow?

    *Satrius.* It is, my lord. Your lordship's answer?

    *Sejanus.*                To what?     185

    *Satrius.* The place, my lord. 'Tis for a gentleman
Your lordship will well like of, when you see him,
And one you may make yours, by the grant.

    *Sejanus.* Well, let him bring his money, and his name.

    *Satrius.* Thank your lordship. He shall, my lord.

    *Sejanus.*               Come hither.   190
Know you this same Eudemus? Is he learned?

173 PREVENTED *forestalled.*
183 FIFTY SESTERTIA *N.*

Act I

    *Satrius.* Reputed so, my lord, and of deep practice.
    *Sejanus.* Bring him in to me in the gallery.
And take you cause to leave us there together.
195 I would confer with him about a grief.—On.
                   *[Exeunt Sejanus, Terentius, Satrius, and Natta.]*
    *Arruntius.* So, yet another? Yet? Oh, desperate state
Of grov'ling honor! Seest thou this, O sun,
And do we see thee after? Methinks day
Should lose his light, when men do lose their shames,
200 And for the empty circumstance of life
Betray their cause of living.
    *Silius.*              Nothing so.
Sejanus can repair if Jove should ruin.
He is the now court god; and well applied
With sacrifice of knees, of crooks, and cringe,
205 He will do more than all the house of heav'n
Can for a thousand hecatombs. 'Tis he
Makes us our day or night. Hell and Elysium
Are in his look. We talk of Rhadamanth,
Furies, and firebrands, but 'tis his frown
210 That is all these, where, on the adverse part,
His smile is more than e'er yet poets feigned
Of bliss, and shades, nectar—
    *Arruntius.*         A serving boy.
I knew him at Caius' trencher, when for hire

192 OF . . . PRACTICE *skilled in plotting.*
195 GRIEF *medical complaint.*
201 NOTHING SO *Not at all.*
203 NOW *present.* APPLIED *applied to.*
208 RHADAMANTH *one of the judges of the underworld.*
210 ON . . . PART *on the other hand.*
212–37 N.
213 CAIUS *Caius Caesar, Augustus' grandson.* TRENCHER *eating platter, hence, table.*

42

He prostituted his abusèd body
To that great gourmand, fat Apicius,                                    215
And was the noted pathic of the time.
   *Sabinus.* And now, the second face of the whole world,
The partner of the empire, hath his image
Reared equal with Tiberius, borne in ensigns;
Commands, disposes every dignity.                                      220
Centurions, tribunes, heads of provinces,
Praetors, and consuls, all that heretofore
Rome's general suffrage gave, is now his sale.
The gain, or rather spoil, of all the earth,
One, and his house, receives.
   *Silius.*                        He hath of late               225
Made him a strength too, strangely, by reducing
All the praetorian bands into one camp,
Which he commands, pretending that the soldier,
By living loose and scattered, fell to riot;
And that if any sudden enterprise                                      230
Should be attempted, their united strength
Would be far more than severed; and their life
More strict, if from the city more removed.
   *Sabinus.* Where now he builds what kind of forts he please,
Is heard to court the soldier by his name,                             235
Woos, feasts the chiefest men of action,
Whose wants, not loves, compel them to be his.

---

235 heard] hard Q,F

215 FAT APICIUS *N.*
216 PATHIC *passive homosexual.*
223 HIS SALE *at his disposal.*
225 ONE . . . HOUSE *one house alone, and that one his.*
226 STRANGELY *by a novel method.* REDUCING *bringing together.*
237 WANTS *necessities.*

And, though he ne'er were liberal by kind,
Yet to his own dark ends, he's most profuse,
240 Lavish, and letting fly he cares not what
To his ambition.
    *Arruntius.*      Yet, hath he ambition?
Is there that step in state can make him higher?
Or more? Or anything he is, but less?
    *Silius.* Nothing but emperor.
    *Arruntius.*          The name Tiberius,
245 I hope, will keep, howe'er he hath forgone
The dignity and power.
    *Silius.*        Sure, while he lives.
    *Arruntius.* And dead, it comes to Drusus. Should he fail,
To the brave issue of Germanicus,
And they are three, too many—ha?—for him
To have a plot upon?
250     *Sabinus.*       I do not know
The heart of his designs, but sure, their face
Looks farther than the present.
    *Arruntius.*        By the gods,
If I could guess he had but such a thought,
My sword should cleave him down from head to heart,
255 But I would find it out; and with my hand
I'd hurl his panting brain about the air,
In mites as small as atomi, to'undo
The knotted bed—
    *Sabinus.*      You are observed, Arruntius.
    *Arruntius. Turns to Sejanus' clients.* Death! I dare tell him so, and
    all his spies.

238 KIND *nature.*
239 TO *in pursuit of.*
244–6 THE NAME . . . POWER *N.*
257 ATOMI *atoms.*
257–8 TO'UNDO . . . BED *to unravel the intricacies of his thoughts.*

44

You, sir, I would, do you look? And you!
   *Sabinus.*                        Forbear.         260
             *[Enter] Satrius [with] Eudemus, [above.]*
   *Satrius.* Here he will instant be. Let's walk a turn.
You're in a muse, Eudemus?
   *Eudemus.*               Not I, sir.
*[Aside.]* I wonder he should mark me out so! Well,
Jove and Apollo form it for the best.
   *Satrius.* Your fortune's made unto you now, Eudemus,     265
If you can but lay hold upon the means.
Do but observe his humor, and—believe it—
He's the noblest Roman, where he takes—
                *[Enter Sejanus.]*
Here comes his lordship.
   *Sejanus.*           Now, good Satrius.
   *Satrius.* This is the gentleman, my lord.
   *Sejanus.*                    Is this?         270
Give me your hand, we must be more acquainted.
Report, sir, hath spoke out your art and learning;
And I am glad I have so needful cause,
However in itself painful and hard,
To make me known to so great virtue. Look,         275
Who's that, Satrius?                  *[Exit Satrius.]*
                I have a grief, sir,
That will desire your help. Your name's Eudemus?
   *Eudemus.* Yes.
   *Sejanus.*      Sir?
   *Eudemus.*         It is, my lord.

261-374 N.
262 IN A MUSE *lost in wonder.*
267 HUMOR *mood.*
278 SIR? . . . LORD *Sejanus prompts Eudemus to show greater respect; Eudemus*
    *takes the hint immediately and addresses Sejanus as " my lord."*

*Sejanus.*                              I hear you are
Physician to Livia, the princess.
280    *Eudemus.* I minister unto her, my good lord.
*Sejanus.* You minister to a royal lady, then.
*Eudemus.* She is, my lord, and fair.
*Sejanus.*                              That's understood
Of all their sex, who are or would be so.
And those that would be, physic soon can make 'em;
285    For those that are, their beauties fear no colors.
*Eudemus.* Your lordship is conceited.
*Sejanus.*                              Sir, you know it,
And can, if need be, read a learnèd lecture
On this and other secrets. Pray you tell me,
What more of ladies, besides Livia,
Have you your patients?
290    *Eudemus.*                  Many, my good lord.
The great Augusta, Urgulania,
Mutilia Prisca and Plancina, divers—
*Sejanus.* And all these tell you the particulars
Of every several grief? How first it grew,
295    And then increased, what action causèd that,
What passion that, and answer to each point
That you will put 'em?
*Eudemus.*            Else, my lord, we know not
How to prescribe the remedies.
*Sejanus.*                  Go to,

---

284 WOULD BE *i.e. beautiful.* PHYSIC *cosmetics.*

285 ARE *i.e. naturally beautiful.* THEIR . . . COLORS *they have no need to fear that their complexions ("colors") will come off at the wrong moment, since they are their own, and hence they need "fear no enemy" of either sex.*

286 CONCEITED *witty, merry.*

294 SEVERAL GRIEF *particular complaint.*

You'are a subtle nation, you physicians!
And grown the only cabinets in court,                    300
To ladies' privacies. Faith, which of these
Is the most pleasant lady in her physic?
Come, you are modest now.
    *Eudemus.*              'Tis fit, my lord.
    *Sejanus.* Why, sir, I do not ask you of their urines,
Whose smell's most violet? Or whose siege is best?       305
Or who makes hardest faces on her stool?
Which lady sleeps with her own face, a-nights?
Which puts her teeth off, with her clothes, in court?
Or which her hair? Which her complexion?
And in which box she puts it? These were questions        310
That might, perhaps, have put your gravity
To some defense of blush. But I inquired
Which was the wittiest? Merriest? Wantonest?
Harmless intergatories, but conceits.
Methinks Augusta should be most perverse,                 315
And froward in her fit.
    *Eudemus.*         She's so, my lord.
    *Sejanus.* I knew it. And Mutilia the most jocund?
    *Eudemus.* 'Tis very true, my lord.
    *Sejanus.*             And why would you
Conceal this from me, now? Come, what's Livia?
I know she's quick, and quaintly spirited,                320

306 her] the Q

---

300 CABINETS *repositories.*
301 PRIVACIES *intimate secrets.*
302 PLEASANT *merry, jocular.*
305 SIEGE *evacuation.*
314 INTERGATORIES *interrogatories.* BUT CONCEITS *merely whims.*
316 HER FIT *the performance of her natural functions.*
320 QUAINTLY *prettily.*

Act I

And will have strange thoughts when she's at leisure.
She tells 'em all to you?
  *Eudemus.*          My noblest lord,
He breathes not in the empire, or on earth,
Whom I would be ambitious to serve
325 In any act that may preserve mine honor,
Before your lordship.
  *Sejanus.*        Sir, you can lose no honor
By trusting aught to me. The coarsest act
Done to my service I can so requite,
As all the world shall style it honorable.
330 Your idle, virtuous definitions
Keep honor poor, and are as scorned as vain.
Those deeds breathe honor that do suck in gain.
  *Eudemus.* But, good my lord, if I should thus betray
The counsels of my patient, and a lady's
335 Of her high place and worth, what might your lordship,
Who presently are to trust me with your own,
Judge of my faith?
  *Sejanus.*        Only the best, I swear.
Say now, that I should utter you my grief,
And with it, the true cause, that it were love,
340 And love to Livia; you should tell her this—
Should she suspect your faith? I would you could
Tell me as much from her. See, if my brain
Could be turned jealous.
  *Eudemus.*        Happily, my lord,
I could in time tell you as much and more,
345 So I might safely promise but the first

323 on] the Q

---

331–2 VAIN . . . GAIN N.
343 JEALOUS *suspicious.* HAPPILY *haply, perhaps.*
345 THE FIRST *the first secret, i.e. that Livia is loved by Sejanus.*

48

To her from you.

   *Sejanus.*        As safely, my Eudemus—
I now dare call thee so—as I have put
The secret into thee.

   *Eudemus.*        My lord—

   *Sejanus.*                Protest not.
Thy looks are vows to me. Use only speed,
And but affect her with Sejanus' love,         350
Thou art a man made to make consuls. Go.

   *Eudemus.* My lord, I'll promise you a private meeting
This day, together.

   *Sejanus.*        Canst thou?

   *Eudemus.*              Yes.

   *Sejanus.*              The place?

   *Eudemus.* My gardens, whither I shall fetch your lordship.

   *Sejanus.* Let me adore my Æsculapius!      355
Why, this indeed is physic! And outspeaks
The knowledge of cheap drugs, or any use
Can be made out of it. More comforting
Than all your opiates, juleps, apozems,
Magistral syrups, or—Begone, my friend,     360
Not barely stylèd, but created so.
Expect things greater than thy largest hopes,
To overtake thee. Fortune shall be taught
To know how ill she hath deserved, thus long
To come behind thy wishes. Go, and speed.    365

                                *[Exit Eudemus.]*

354 shall fetch your lordship] shall your lordship F

350 AFFECT *acquaint, arouse interest in.*
355 ÆSCULAPIUS *god of medicine.*
356 OUTSPEAKS *surpasses.*
359 APOZEMS *infusions.*
360 MAGISTRAL *sovereign.*

Act I

Ambition makes more trusty slaves than need.
These fellows, by the favor of their art,
Have still the means to tempt, ofttimes the power.
If Livia will be now corrupted, then
370  Thou hast the way, Sejanus, to work out
His secrets, who (thou knowest) endures thee not,
Her husband Drusus, and to work against them.
Prosper it, Pallas, thou that better'st wit;
For Venus hath the smallest share in it.
       [Enter] Tiberius [and] Drusus, [attended.]
    Tiberius. (One kneels to him.) We not endure these flatteries.
375      Let him stand.
Our empire, ensigns, axes, rods, and state
Take not away our human nature from us.
Look up on us, and fall before the gods.
    Sejanus. How like a god speaks Caesar!
    Arruntius. [Aside.]                        There, observe!
380  He can endure that second, that's no flattery.
Oh, what is it proud slime will not believe
Of his own worth, to hear it equal praised
Thus with the gods?
    Cotta. [Aside.]        He did not hear it, sir.

383 *Cotta*] COR. Q,F *N.*
---
368 STILL *always.*
370 WORK OUT *uncover,* "*worm out.*"
373 BETTER'ST *enhancest.*
375–8 WE NOT . . . GODS *N.*
375 NOT *do not.*
376 AXES, RODS *the fasces, bundles of rods bound up with axes in the middle,
       their blades projecting, carried before the high magistrates as symbols of
       authority.*
378 LOOK . . . US *Look us in the face.*
380 SECOND *follower.*
382 HIS *its.*

50

*Arruntius.* He did not? Tut, he must not; we think meanly.
'Tis your most courtly, known confederacy, 385
To have your private parasite redeem
What he, in public subtlety, will lose
To making him a name.
*Haterius.* Right mighty lord—
[*Gives him letters.*]
*Tiberius.* We must make up our ears 'gainst these assaults
Of charming tongues. We pray you use no more 390
These contumelies to us. Style not us
Or lord, or mighty, who profess ourself
The servant of the Senate, and are proud
T'enjoy them our good, just, and favoring lords.
*Cordus.* [*Aside.*] Rarely dissembled!
*Arruntius.* Princelike, to the life. 395
*Sabinus.* When power, that may command, so much descends,
Their bondage, whom it stoops to, it intends.
*Tiberius.* Whence are these letters?
*Haterius.* From the Senate.
*Tiberius.* So.
[*Latiaris gives him letters.*]
Whence these?
*Latiaris.* From thence too.
*Tiberius.* Are they sitting now?
*Latiaris.* They stay thy answer, Caesar.
*Silius.* If this man 400

385–8 N.
389 MAKE UP *defend, place guards about.*
394 ENJOY *have.*
396–7 WHEN . . . INTENDS *When those in power put on such an exaggerated
    show of humility, it can only mean that they are planning to enslave those
    to whom they are humbling themselves.*
399 STAY *await.*

51

Had but a mind allied unto his words,
How blest a fate were it to us, and Rome!
We could not think that state for which to change,
Although the aim were our old liberty.
405 The ghosts of those that fell for that would grieve
Their bodies lived not, now, again to serve.
Men are deceived who think there can be thrall
Beneath a virtuous prince. Wished liberty
Ne'er lovelier looks than under such a crown.
410 But when his grace is merely but lip-good,
And that, no longer than he airs himself
Abroad in public, there to seem to shun
The strokes and stripes of flatterers, which within
Are lechery unto him, and so feed
415 His brutish sense with their afflicting sound,
As, dead to virtue, he permits himself
Be carried like a pitcher, by the ears,
To every act of vice: this is a case
Deserves our fear, and doth presage the nigh
420 And close approach of blood and tyranny.
Flattery is midwife unto princes' rage,
And nothing sooner doth help forth a tyrant
Than that and whisperers' grace, who have the time,
The place, the power, to make all men offenders.
425 *Arruntius.* He should be told this, and be bid dissemble
With fools and blind men. We that know the evil

402 were] where Q

403 THINK *imagine, conceive.*   CHANGE *exchange.*
413 WITHIN *inwardly.*
414 LECHERY *voluptuous pleasure.*
415 AFFLICTING *capable of lashing his "brutish sense" awake.*
423 WHISPERERS' GRACE *indulgence granted informers.*

Should hunt the palace rats, or give them bane,
Fright hence these worse than ravens, that devour
The quick, where they but prey upon the dead.
He shall be told it.

    *Sabinus.*         Stay, Arruntius,          430
We must abide our opportunity,
And practice what is fit, as what is needful.
It is not safe t'enforce a sovereign's ear.
Princes hear well, if they at all will hear.

    *Arruntius.* Ha! Say you so? Well, in the meantime, Jove—   435
Say not but I do call upon thee now—
Of all wild beasts, preserve me from a tyrant,
And of all tame, a flatterer.

    *Silius.*              'Tis well prayed.

    *Tiberius.* Return the lords this voice: we are their creature,
And it is fit a good and honest prince,          440
Whom they, out of their bounty, have instructed
With so dilate and absolute a power,
Should owe the office of it to their service,
And good of all and every citizen.
Nor shall it e'er repent us to have wished          445
The Senate just and fav'ring lords unto us,
Since their free loves do yield no less defense
T'a prince's state, than his own innocence.
Say then there can be nothing in their thought
Shall want to please us, that hath pleasèd them.       450
Our suffrage rather shall prevent, than stay

427 BANE *rat poison.*
429 QUICK *living.* THEY *i.e. the ravens.*
431 ABIDE *await.*
441 INSTRUCTED *provided.*
442 DILATE *extended.*
450 WANT *fail.*
451 PREVENT *anticipate.*

Behind their wills. 'Tis empire to obey
Where such, so great, so grave, so good determine.
Yet, for the suit of Spain t'erect a temple
455 In honor of our mother and ourself,
We must, with pardon of the Senate, not
Assent thereto. Their lordships may object
Our not denying the same late request
Unto the Asian cities. We desire
460 That our defense for suffering that be known
In these brief reasons, with our afterpurpose:
Since deified Augustus hindered not
A temple to be built at Pergamum,
In honor of himself and sacred Rome,
465 We, that have all his deeds and words observed
Ever, in place of laws, the rather followed
That pleasing precedent, because, with ours,
The Senate's reverence also there was joined.
But as, t'have once received it, may deserve
470 The gain of pardon, so to be adored
With the continued style and note of gods,
Through all the provinces, were wild ambition,
And no less pride. Yea, ev'n Augustus' name
Would early vanish, should it be profaned
475 With such promiscuous flatteries. For our part,
We here protest it, and are covetous
Posterity should know it, we are mortal,
And can but deeds of men. 'Twere glory' enough,
Could we be truly a prince. And they shall add
480 Abounding grace unto our memory
That shall report us worthy our forefathers,

454–502 N.
471 NOTE *manner of address.*
478 CAN *can do.*

Careful of your affairs, constant in dangers,
And not afraid of any private frown
For public good. These things shall be to us
Temples and statues rearèd in your minds,                    485
The fairest and most during imag'ry.
For those of stone or brass, if they become
Odious in judgment of posterity,
Are more contemned as dying sepulchers
Than ta'en for living monuments. We then                     490
Make here our suit, alike to gods and men,
The one, until the period of our race,
T'inspire us with a free and quiet mind,
Discerning both divine and human laws;
The other, to vouchsafe us after death                       495
An honorable mention, and fair praise,
T'accompany our actions and our name.
The rest of greatness princes may command,
And therefore may neglect. Only a long,
A lasting, high, and happy memory                            500
They should, without being satisfied, pursue.
Contempt of fame begets contempt of virtue.

   *Natta.* Rare!

   *Satrius.*      Most divine!

   *Sejanus.*              The oracles are ceased,
That only Caesar, with their tongue, might speak.

   *Arruntius.* Let me be gone; most felt and open this!      505

   *Cordus.* Stay.

   *Arruntius.*      What? To hear more cunning and fine words,

---

492 PERIOD ... RACE *end of our life.*
493 FREE *honorable, magnanimous.*
503 ORACLES ARE CEASED *N.*
505 FELT *palpable, gross.* OPEN *obvious.*

Act I

With their sound flattered ere their sense be meant?
   *Tiberius.* Their choice of Antium, there to place the gift
Vowed to the goddess for our mother's health,
510 We will the Senate know we fairly like;
As also of their grant to Lepidus
For his repairing the Æmilian place,
And restoration of those monuments.
Their grace too in confining of Silanus
515 To th'other isle Cythera, at the suit
Of his religious sister, much commends
Their policy so tempered with their mercy.
But for the honors which they have decreed
To our Sejanus, to advance his statue
520 In Pompey's theater, whose ruining fire
His vigilance and labor kept restrained
In that one loss, they have therein outgone
Their own great wisdoms, by their skillful choice,
And placing of their bounties on a man
525 Whose merit more adorns the dignity
Than that can him, and gives a benefit
In taking, greater than it can receive.
Blush not, Sejanus, thou great aid of Rome,
Associate of our labors, our chief helper.
530 Let us not force thy simple modesty

---

507 THEIR . . . MEANT *praised for their sound despite their obvious insincerity.*
508 ANTIUM *the present port of Anzio.*
508–9 GIFT . . . GODDESS "Fortuna Equestris," *explains Jonson marginally, referring to an equestrian statue of the Goddess Fortuna, donated by the Roman knights as an offering for the dowager empress' health.*
511–3 *N.*
514–6 CONFINING . . . SISTER *N.*
519 ADVANCE *erect.*
520 POMPEY'S THEATER *N.*

With off'ring at thy praise, for more we cannot,
Since there's no voice can take it. No man here
Receive our speeches as hyperboles,
For we are far from flattering our friend,
Let envy know, as from the need to flatter.                535
Nor let them ask the causes of our praise.
Princes have still their grounds reared with themselves,
Above the poor low flats of common men,
And who will search the reasons of their acts
Must stand on equal bases. Lead, away.                     540
Our loves unto the Senate.
      [*Exeunt Tiberius, Sejanus, Natta, Haterius, Latiaris, etc.*]
  *Arruntius.*          Caesar!
  *Sabinus.*                Peace.
  *Cordus.* Great Pompey's theater was never ruined
Till now, that proud Sejanus hath a statue
Reared on his ashes.
  *Arruntius.*        Place the shame of soldiers
Above the best of generals? Crack the world!            545
And bruise the name of Romans into dust,
Ere we behold it!
  *Silius.*         Check your passion.
Lord Drusus tarries.
  *Drusus.*        Is my father mad?
Weary of life and rule, lords? Thus to heave
An idol up with praise, make him his mate,                550

531 off'ring at *attempting.*
531-2 more . . . it *We can do no more than feebly attempt it, since no voice, not even our own, could really accomplish it.*
537-8 princes . . . men *Princes have always occupied an elevation of their own, above the low ground inhabited by ordinary men.*
539 who *those who.*
548-59 N.

Act I

His rival in the empire!
   *Arruntius.*            Oh, good prince!
   *Drusus.* Allow him statues? Titles? Honors such
As he himself refuseth?
   *Arruntius.*         Brave, brave Drusus!
   *Drusus.* The first ascents to sovereignty are hard,
555  But entered once, there never wants or means
Or ministers, to help th'aspirer on.
   *Arruntius.* True, gallant Drusus.
   *Drusus.*               We must shortly pray
To Modesty, that he will rest contented—
   *Arruntius.* Aye, where he is, and not write emperor.
   [*Re-enter*] *Sejanus,* [*Satrius, Latiaris,*] *followed with clients, etc.*
560  *Sejanus.* [*to Satrius.*] There is your bill, and yours. Bring you
     your man.
I'have moved for you, too, Latiaris.
   *Drusus.*              What?
Is your vast greatness grown so blindly bold,
That you will over us?
   *Sejanus.*       Why, then give way.
   *Drusus.* Give way, Colossus? Do you lift? Advance you?
Take that!        *Drusus strikes him.*
565  *Arruntius.* Good! Brave! Excellent brave prince!
   *Drusus.* Nay, come, approach. [*Draws his sword.*] What? Stand
     you off? At gaze?

---

551 RIVAL *partner.*
555 OR *either.*
559 WRITE *claim the title of.*
560–75 N.
561 MOVED FOR YOU *spoken in your behalf.*
564 LIFT *rear up.*
566 AT GAZE *eyeing me (?)*

It looks too full of death for thy cold spirits.
Avoid mine eye, dull camel, or my sword
Shall make thy brav'ry fitter for a grave
Than for a triumph. I'll advance a statue                    570
O' your own bulk, but't shall be on the cross,
Where I will nail your pride at breadth and length,
And crack those sinews, which are yet but stretched
With your swol'n fortune's rage.
    *Arruntius.*                    A noble prince!
    *All.* A Castor, a Castor, a Castor, a Castor!            575
        [*Exeunt all but Sejanus.*]
    *Sejanus.* He that with such wrong moved, can bear it through
With patience, and an even mind, knows how
To turn it back. Wrath, covered, carries fate.
Revenge is lost if I profess my hate.
What was my practice late, I'll now pursue                   580
As my fell justice. This hath styled it new.         [*Exit.*]

                *Chorus of Musicians.*

567 spirits] spirit Q
_____

569 BRAV'RY *greatness.*
575 A CASTOR *N.*
577 EVEN *unperturbed.*
578 TURN IT BACK *retaliate.*
579 PROFESS *proclaim.*
580–1 WHAT . . . NEW *My intriguing against Drusus will now continue as
    implacable revenge. This incident has merely given it a new name. N.*

# Act II

[*The garden of Eudemus. Enter*] *Sejanus, Livia,* [*and*] *Eudemus.*

*Sejanus.* Physician, thou art worthy of a province,
For the great favors done unto our loves.
And but that greatest Livia bears a part
In the requital of thy services,
5   I should alone despair of aught like means,
To give them worthy satisfaction.
   *Livia.* Eudemus, I will see it, shall receive
A fit and full reward for his large merit.
But for this potion we intend to Drusus,
10   No more our husband now, whom shall we choose
As the most apt and abled instrument
To minister it to him?
   *Eudemus.*             I say Lygdus.
   *Sejanus.* Lygdus? What's he?
   *Livia.*                 An eunuch Drusus loves.
   *Eudemus.* Aye, and his cupbearer.
   *Sejanus.*               Name not a second.
15   If Drusus love him, and he have that place,
We cannot think a fitter.
   *Eudemus.*           True, my lord,

5 AUGHT LIKE *to any degree sufficient.*

60

For free access and trust are two main aids.
   *Sejanus.* Skillful physician!
   *Livia.*                 But he must be wrought
To th'undertaking, with some labored art.
   *Sejanus.* Is he ambitious?
   *Livia.*             No.
   *Sejanus.*           Or covetous?            20
   *Livia.* Neither.
   *Eudemus.*      Yet gold is a good general charm.
   *Sejanus.* What is he then?
   *Livia.*              Faith, only wanton, light.
   *Sejanus.* How! Is he young? And fair?
   *Eudemus.*             A delicate youth.
   *Sejanus.* Send him to me, I'll work him. Royal lady,
Though I have loved you long, and with that height     25
Of zeal and duty—like the fire, which more
It mounts, it trembles—thinking nought could add
Unto the fervor which your eye had kindled;
Yet now I see your wisdom, judgment, strength,
Quickness, and will to apprehend the means     30
To your own good and greatness, I protest
Myself through-rarefied, and turned all flame
In your affection. Such a spirit as yours
Was not created for the idle second
To a poor flash as Drusus, but to shine     35
Bright as the moon among the lesser lights,
And share the sov'reignty of all the world.
Then Livia triumphs in her proper sphere,

18 WROUGHT *persuaded.*
24 WORK *induce.*
32 THROUGH-RAREFIED *wholly turned to spirit.*
34 SECOND *follower.*
35 POOR FLASH *creature of a moment's brightness.*

Act II

When she and her Sejanus shall divide
40 The name of Caesar, and Augusta's star
Be dimmed with glory of a brighter beam;
When Agrippina's fires are quite extinct,
And the scarce seen Tiberius borrows all
His little light from us, whose folded arms
Shall make one perfect orb. [*Knocking within.*] Who's that?
45 Eudemus,
Look. [*Exit Eudemus.*] 'Tis not Drusus? Lady, do not fear.
    *Livia.* Not I, my lord. My fear and love of him
Left me at once.
    *Sejanus.*         Illustrous lady! Stay—
*Eudemus.* [*Within.*] I'll tell his lordship.

                              [*Re-enter Eudemus.*]
    *Sejanus.*                      Who is't, Eudemus?
50 *Eudemus.* One of your lordship's servants brings you word
The emp'ror hath sent for you.
    *Sejanus.*                Oh! Where is he?
With your fair leave, dear princess, I'll but ask
A question, and return.                          *He goes out.*
    *Eudemus.*         Fortunate princess!
How are you blest in the fruition
55 Of this unequaled man, this soul of Rome,
The empire's life, and voice of Caesar's world!
    *Livia.* So blessèd, my Eudemus, as to know
The bliss I have, with what I ought to owe
The means that wrought it. How do I look today?

40 AUGUSTA *Livia, widow of Augustus, Tiberius' mother, still alive at the time
    of the play's action, and still a powerful influence on her son.*
44 FOLDED ARMS *in an embrace.*
48 AT ONCE *at the same time.* ILLUSTROUS *illustrious.*
54 FRUITION *enjoying.*
59 MEANS . . . IT *the agent who brought it about, i.e. Eudemus himself.*

*Eudemus.* Excellent clear, believe it. This same fucus                    60
Was well laid on.
    *Livia.*                Methinks 'tis here not white.
    *Eudemus.* Lend me your scarlet, lady. 'Tis the sun
Hath giv'n some little taint unto the ceruse.
You should have used of the white oil I gave you.
Sejanus for your love! His very name                                       65
Commandeth above Cupid, or his shafts—

                                        [*Paints her cheeks.*]

    *Livia.* Nay, now yo'have made it worse.
    *Eudemus.*                        I'll help it straight—
And, but pronounced, is a sufficient charm
Against all rumor, and of absolute power
To satisfy for any lady's honor.                                           70
    *Livia.* What do you now, Eudemus?
    *Eudemus.*                    Make a light fucus,
To touch you o'er withal.—Honored Sejanus!
What act, though ne'er so strange and insolent,
But that addition will at least bear out,
If't do not expiate?
    *Livia.*        Here, good physician.                                  75
    *Eudemus.* I like this study to preserve the love
Of such a man, that comes not every hour
To greet the world—'Tis now well, lady, you should
Use of the dentifrice I prescribed you, too,
To clear your teeth, and the prepared pomatum,                             80
To smooth the skin.—A lady cannot be

60 CLEAR *of clear complexion.* FUCUS *cosmetic paint.*
63 CERUSE *a white lead cosmetic.*
73 INSOLENT *unaccustomed.*
74 ADDITION *title.* BEAR OUT *lend support to.*
80 POMATUM *pomade, scented ointment.*

Act II

Too curious of her form, that still would hold
The heart of such a person, made her captive,
As you have his; who, to endear him more
85    In your clear eye, hath put away his wife,
The trouble of his bed and your delights,
Fair Apicata, and made spacious room
To your new pleasures.
    *Livia.*                      Have not we returned
That, with our hate of Drusus, and discovery
Of all his counsels?
90    *Eudemus.*            Yes, and wisely, lady.
The ages that succeed, and stand far off
To gaze at your high prudence, shall admire
And reckon it an act without your sex,
It hath that rare appearance. Some will think
95    Your fortune could not yield a deeper sound
Than mixed with Drusus, but when they shall hear
That, and the thunder of Sejanus meet—
Sejanus, whose high name doth strike the stars,
And rings about the concave, great Sejanus,
100    Whose glories, style, and titles are himself—
The often iterating of Sejanus,
They then will lose their thoughts, and be ashamed
To take acquaintance of them.

                              [*Re-enter Sejanus.*]

    *Sejanus.*                  I must make
A rude departure, lady. Caesar sends
105    With all his haste both of command and prayer.
Be resolute in our plot. You have my soul

82 CURIOUS *careful.*
85 CLEAR *bright.*
93 WITHOUT *beyond.*
99 CONCAVE *vault of heaven.*

64

As certain yours as it is my body's.
And, wise physician, so prepare the poison
As you may lay the subtle operation
Upon some natural disease of his.                                    110
Your eunuch send to me. I kiss your hands,
Glory of ladies, and commend my love
To your best faith and memory.
    *Livia.*                My lord,
I shall but change your words. Farewell. Yet this
Remember for your heed: he loves you not.                            115
You know what I have told you; his designs
Are full of grudge and danger. We must use
More than a common speed.
    *Sejanus.*          Excellent lady,
How you do fire my blood!
    *Livia.*            Well, you must go?
The thoughts be best, are least set forth to show.                   120

                                [*Exit Sejanus.*]

    *Eudemus.* When will you take some physic, lady?
    *Livia.*                    When
I shall, Eudemus. But let Drusus' drug
Be first prepared.
    *Eudemus.*    Were Lygdus made, that's done.
I have it ready. And tomorrow morning
I'll send you a perfume, first to resolve                            125
And procure sweat, and then prepare a bath
To cleanse and clear the cutis, against when
I'll have an excellent new fucus made,
Resistive 'gainst the sun, the rain, or wind,

114 CHANGE *give you back.*
121–2 WHEN I SHALL *When it pleases me* (?)
123 MADE *won to our purpose.*
127 CUTIS *skin.* AGAINST WHEN *in anticipation of which.*

130 Which you shall lay on with a breath, or oil,
As you best like, and last some fourteen hours.
This change came timely, lady, for your health,
And the restoring your complexion,
Which Drusus' choler had almost burnt up;
135 Wherein your fortune hath prescribed you better
Than art could do.

    *Livia.*         Thanks, good physician.
I'll use my fortune, you shall see, with reverence.
Is my coach ready?

    *Eudemus.*        It attends your highness.       *[Exeunt.]*

    *[An apartment in the palace. Enter]* Sejanus.

    *Sejanus.* If this be not revenge, when I have done
140 And made it perfect, let Egyptian slaves,
Parthians, and barefoot Hebrews brand my face,
And print my body full of injuries.
Thou lost thyself, child Drusus, when thou thought'st
Thou couldst outskip my vengeance, or outstand
145 The power I had to crush thee into air.
Thy follies now shall taste what kind of man
They have provoked, and this thy father's house
Crack in the flame of my incensèd rage,
Whose fury shall admit no shame or mean.
150 Adultery? It is the lightest ill
I will commit. A race of wicked acts
Shall flow out of my anger, and o'erspread
The world's wide face, which no posterity

130 LAY ON *apply.*
134 CHOLER *fiery disposition.*
136 ART *i.e. of the physician.*
139–40 EGYPTIAN SLAVES . . . PARTHIANS . . . HEBREWS *symbols of servitude and*
    *abjection.*

Shall e'er approve, nor yet keep silent—things

That for their cunning, close and cruel mark,                    155

Thy father would wish his, and shall, perhaps,

Carry the empty name, but we the prize.

On then, my soul, and start not in thy course.

Though heav'n drop sulphur and hell belch out fire,

Laugh at the idle terrors. Tell proud Jove,                      160

Between his power and thine there is no odds.

'Twas only fear first in the world made gods.

                [*Enter Tiberius, attended.*]

  *Tiberius.* Is yet Sejanus come?

  *Sejanus.*                 He's here, dread Caesar.

  *Tiberius.* Let all depart that chamber, and the next.

                    [*Exeunt Attendants.*]

Sit down, my comfort. When the master prince                     165

Of all the world, Sejanus, saith he fears,

Is it not fatal?

  *Sejanus.*    Yes, to those are feared.

  *Tiberius.* And not to him?

  *Sejanus.*             Not if he wisely turn

That part of fate he holdeth, first on them.

  *Tiberius.* That nature, blood, and laws of kind forbid.      170

  *Sejanus.* Do policy and state forbid it?

  *Tiberius.*               No.

  *Sejanus.* The rest of poor respects, then, let go by.

State is enough to make th'act just, them guilty.

  *Tiberius.* Long hate pursues such acts.

  *Sejanus.*                 Whom hatred frights,

Let him not dream on sov'reignty.

---

156–7 SHALL . . . PRIZE *may perhaps be reputed to have done the deeds, but I
      alone will profit from them.*

170 KIND *kinship.*

173 STATE *political reasons.*

67

175    *Tiberius.*                     Are rites
Of faith, love, piety, to be trod down?
Forgotten? And made vain?
    *Sejanus.*               All for a crown.
The prince who shames a tyrant's name to bear,
Shall never dare do anything but fear.
180 All the command of scepters quite doth perish
If it begin religious thoughts to cherish.
Whole empires fall, swayed by those nice respects.
It is the license of dark deeds protects
Ev'n states most hated, when no laws resist
185 The sword, but that it acteth what it list.
    *Tiberius.* Yet so, we may do all things cruelly,
Not safely.
    *Sejanus.* Yes, and do them thoroughly.
    *Tiberius.* Knows yet Sejanus whom we point at?
    *Sejanus.*                         Aye,
Or else my thought, my sense, or both do err.
'Tis Agrippina?
190    *Tiberius.*       She, and her proud race.
    *Sejanus.* Proud? Dangerous, Caesar. For in them apace
The father's spirit shoots up. Germanicus
Lives in their looks, their gait, their form, t'upbraid us
With his close death, if not revenge the same.
    *Tiberius.* The act's not known.
195    *Sejanus.*                Not proved. But whisp'ring fame

---

187 thoroughly] throughly Q

---

182 NICE *squeamish.*
188 AYE *N.*
194 CLOSE *secretly managed.*
195 FAME *rumor.*

Knowledge and proof doth to the jealous give,
Who, than to fail, would their own thought believe.
It is not safe the children draw long breath,
That are provokèd by a parent's death.

    *Tiberius.* It is as dangerous to make them hence,         200
If nothing but their birth be their offense.

    *Sejanus.* Stay till they strike at Caesar. Then their crime
Will be enough, but late, and out of time
For him to punish.

    *Tiberius.*         Do they purpose it?

    *Sejanus.* You know, sir, thunder speaks not till it hit.      205
Be not secure; none swiftlier are oppressed
Than they whom confidence betrays to rest.
Let not your daring make your danger such.
All power's to be feared, where 'tis too much.
The youths are, of themselves, hot, violent,            210
Full of great thought; and that male-spirited dame,
Their mother, slacks no means to put them on,
By large allowance, popular presentings,
Increase of train and state, suing for titles;
Hath them commended with like prayers, like vows,      215
To the same gods, with Caesar. Days and nights
She spends in banquets and ambitious feasts
For the nobility, where Caius Silius,
Titius Sabinus, old Arruntius,

196 JEALOUS *suspicious.*
197 WHO . . . BELIEVE "*I.e., who rather than fail of proof, would believe the mere evidence of their own thoughts*" (*Whalley, quoted in Herford and Simpson, 9,608*).
200 MAKE THEM HENCE *put them out of the way.*
206 SECURE *overconfident, careless.*
207 BETRAYS . . . REST *lulls into false security.*
213 ALLOWANCE *approbation, permission, and, perhaps also, money.* POPULAR PRESENTINGS *presenting them to the populace.*

Act II

220  Asinius Gallus, Furnius, Regulus,
     And others of that discontented list
     Are the prime guests. There, and to these she tells
     Whose niece she was, whose daughter, and whose wife.
     And then must they compare her with Augusta,
225  Aye, and prefer her too, commend her form,
     Extol her fruitfulness; at which a show'r
     Falls for the memory of Germanicus,
     Which they blow over straight with windy praise
     And puffing hopes of her aspiring sons;
230  Who, with these hourly ticklings, grow so pleased
     And wantonly conceited of themselves,
     As now they stick not to believe they're such
     As these do give 'em out; and would be thought
     More than competitors, immediate heirs.
235  Whilst to their thirst of rule they win the rout
     That's still the friend of novelty, with hope
     Of future freedom, which on every change
     That greedily, though emptily, expects.
     Caesar, 'tis age in all things breeds neglects,
240  And princes that will keep old dignity
     Must not admit too youthful heirs stand by—
     Not their own issue, but so darkly set
     As shadows are in picture, to give height
     And luster to themselves.

223 NIECE *granddaughter.*
226 SHOW'R *of tears.*
230 TICKLINGS *incitements.*
232 STICK *hesitate.*
234 COMPETITORS . . . HEIRS *i.e. of the empire.* N.
235 ROUT *mob.*
238 THAT *the rout.* EXPECTS *awaits.*
242-3 BUT . . . PICTURE *unless they remain dark, like background shadows in
     paintings.*

    *Tiberius.*               We will command
Their rank thoughts down, and with a stricter hand        245
Than we have yet put forth, their trains must bate,
Their titles, feasts, and factions.
    *Sejanus.*               Or your state.
But how, sir, will you work?
    *Tiberius.*             Confine 'em.
    *Sejanus.*                   No.
They are too great, and that too faint a blow
To give them now. It would have served at first,        250
When, with the weakest touch, their knot had burst.
But now your care must be not to detect
The smallest cord or line of your suspect.
For such who know the weight of princes' fear
Will, when they find themselves discovered, rear        255
Their forces, like seen snakes, that else would lie
Rolled in their circles, close. Nought is more high,
Daring, or desperate, than offenders found.
Where guilt is, rage and courage both abound.
The course must be to let 'em still swell up,        260
Riot and surfeit on blind Fortune's cup;
Give 'em more place, more dignities, more style;
Call 'em to court, to Senate; in the while,
Take from their strength some one or twain or more

---

259 both] doth F

245 RANK *puffed up, swollen, rebellious.*
246 BATE *reduce.*
252 DETECT *reveal.*
253 SUSPECT *suspicion.*
257 ROLLED . . . CLOSE *coiled up tightly.* HIGH *audacious.*
261 BLIND FORTUNE *the goddess Fortuna, mistress of affairs on earth, traditionally*
      *represented as blind and hence only able to allot her favors haphazardly.*
262 PLACE *status.*

265 Of the main fautors—it will fright the store—
And by some by-occasion. Thus, with sleight
You shall disarm them first, and they, in night
Of their ambition, not perceive the train,
Till in the engine they are caught and slain.

270     *Tiberius.* We would not kill if we knew how to save;
Yet, than a throne, 'tis cheaper give a grave.
Is there no way to bind them by deserts?
    *Sejanus.* Sir, wolves do change their hair, but not their hearts.
While thus your thought unto a mean is tied,

275 You neither dare enough, nor do provide.
All modesty is fond, and chiefly where
The subject is no less compelled to bear
Than praise his sov'reign's acts.
    *Tiberius.*                                We can no longer
Keep on our mask to thee, our dear Sejanus.

280 Thy thoughts are ours in all, and we but proved
Their voice, in our designs, which by assenting
Hath more confirmed us than if heart'ning Jove
Had, from his hundred statues, bid us strike,

---

267 disarm them first] disarm first F

---

265 FAUTORS *partisans.* STORE *group.*
266 BY-OCCASION *side issue.*
267–8 IN NIGHT . . . AMBITION *their minds darkened by ambition.*
268 TRAIN *ruse.*
269 ENGINE *trap.*
273 WOLVES . . . HEARTS *a Greek proverb.*
274 A MEAN *a moderate course.*
275 PROVIDE *exercise foresight.*
276 MODESTY *moderation.* FOND *foolish.*
276–8 CHIEFLY . . . ACTS *especially when the subject must not only suffer from
        his ruler's acts, but praise them at the same time.*
280 PROVED *tested.*
282 HEART'NING *encouraging.*

And at the stroke clicked all his marble thumbs.
But who shall first be struck?

   *Sejanus.*              First Caius Silius.       285
He is the most of mark, and most of danger,
In power and reputation equal strong,
Having commanded an imperial army
Seven years together, vanquished Sacrovir
In Germany, and thence obtained to wear       290
The ornaments triumphal. His steep fall,
By how much it doth give the weightier crack,
Will send more wounding terror to the rest,
Command them stand aloof, and give more way
To our surprising of the principal.       295

   *Tiberius.* But what, Sabinus?

   *Sejanus.*              Let him grow awhile;
His fate is not yet ripe. We must not pluck
At all together, lest we catch ourselves.
And there's Arruntius too, he only talks.
But Sosia, Silius' wife, would be wound in       300
Now, for she hath a fury in her breast
More than hell ever knew, and would be sent
Thither in time. Then is there one Cremutius
Cordus, a writing fellow they have got
To gather notes of the precedent times,       305

284 CLICKED . . . THUMBS *in the manner of the crowds at a gladiatorial contest, turning their thumbs down or up to signify death or mercy for the fallen combatant.*
285–95 N.
289 SACROVIR *Gallic general who led a revolt against Rome in A.D. 21*
294–5 AND GIVE . . . PRINCIPAL *and ease our job of taking our chief enemies by surprise.*
300, 302 WOULD BE *should be.*
303 THITHER *i.e. to hell.*
305 NOTES *observations.*

Act II

And make them into annals—a most tart
And bitter spirit, I hear, who under color
Of praising those, doth tax the present state,
Censures the men, the actions, leaves no trick,
310  No practice unexamined, parallels
The times, the governments, a pròfessed champion
For the old liberty—
    *Tiberius.*         A perishing wretch!
As if there were that chaos bred in things,
That laws and liberty would not rather choose
315  To be quite broken and ta'en hence by us,
Than have the stain to be preserved by such.
Have we the means to make these guilty first?
    *Sejanus.* Trust that to me. Let Caesar, by his power,
But cause a formal meeting of the Senate;
320  I will have matter and accusers ready.
    *Tiberius.* But how? Let us consult.
    *Sejanus.*               We shall misspend
The time of action. Counsels are unfit
In business, where all rest is more pernicious
Than rashness can be. Acts of this close kind
325  Thrive more by execution than advice.
There is no ling'ring in that work begun,
Which cannot praisèd be, until through done.
    *Tiberius.* Our edict shall forthwith command a court.
While I can live, I will prevent earth's fury:

308 THOSE "*the precedent times.*"
309 CENSURES *judges.*
312 PERISHING *ruinous.*
313–16 AS IF . . . SUCH *N.*
323 REST *inaction.*
324 CLOSE *secretive.*
326–7 THERE IS . . . DONE *Delay is intolerable in the kind of job that cannot be
praised until it is finished (because until then it cannot be seen).*

74

Ἐμοῦ θανόντος γαῖα μιχθήτω πυρί.                    [*Exit.*]  330
              [*Enter*] *Posthumus.*

*Posthumus.* My lord Sejanus—
*Sejanus.*                              Julius Posthumus,
Come with my wish! What news from Agrippina's?
*Posthumus.* Faith, none. They all lock up themselves a'late,
Or talk in character. I have not seen
A company so changed. Except they had                        335
Intelligence by augury'of our practice.
*Sejanus.* When were you there?
*Posthumus.*                            Last night.
*Sejanus.*                                      And what guests found you?
*Posthumus.* Sabinus, Silius—the old list—Arruntius,
Furnius, and Gallus.
*Sejanus.*              Would not these talk?
*Posthumus.*                                      Little.
And yet we offered choice of argument,                        340
Satrius was with me.
*Sejanus.*              Well, 'tis guilt enough
Their often meeting. You forgot t'extol
The hospitable lady?
*Posthumus.*          No, that trick
Was well put home, and had succeeded too,
But that Sabinus coughed a caution out,                       345
For she began to swell.
*Sejanus.*                And may she burst!
Julius, I would have you go instantly
Unto the palace of the great Augusta,

330 "*When I am dead, let fire overwhelm the earth.*"
334 CHARACTER *code.*
335 EXCEPT *unless.*
340 ARGUMENT *topic of conversation.*
342–3 T'EXTOL . . . LADY *N.*

And, by your kindest friend, get swift access.
350 Acquaint her with these meetings. Tell the words
You brought me th'other day of Silius.
Add somewhat to 'em. Make her understand
The danger of Sabinus, and the times,
Out of his closeness. Give Arruntius words
355 Of malice against Caesar, so to Gallus,
But above all to Agrippina. Say,
As you may truly, that her infinite pride,
Propped with the hopes of her too fruitful womb,
With popular studies gapes for sov'reignty,
360 And threatens Caesar. Pray Augusta then,
That for her own, great Caesar's, and the pub-
lic safety she be pleased to urge these dangers.
Caesar is too secure; he must be told;
And best he'll take it from a mother's tongue.
365 Alas, what is't for us to sound, t'explore,
To watch, oppose, plot, practice, or prevent,
If he, for whom it is so strongly labored,
Shall, out of greatness and free spirit, be
Supinely negligent? Our city's now
370 Divided as in time o'th'civil war,
And men forbear not to declare themselves
Of Agrippina's party. Every day
The faction multiplies, and will do more
If not resisted. You can best enlarge it
375 As you find audience. Noble Posthumus,
Commend me to your Prisca, and pray her

349 YOUR KINDEST FRIEND N.
354 GIVE attribute to.
359 POPULAR STUDIES courting of the populace.
361–2 PUB-/LIC N.
369–72 N.
374 ENLARGE IT amplify the theme.

She will solicit this great business
To earnest and most present execution,
With all her utmost credit with Augusta.
   *Posthumus.* I shall not fail in my instructions.      [*Exit.*]   380
   *Sejanus.* This second, from his mother, will well urge
Our late design, and spur on Caesar's rage,
Which else might grow remiss. The way to put
A prince in blood, is to present the shapes
Of dangers greater than they are, like late               385
Or early shadows, and sometimes to feign
Where there are none, only to make him fear.
His fear will make him cruel, and once entered,
He doth not easily learn to stop, or spare
Where he may doubt. This have I made my rule,       390
To thrust Tiberius into tyranny,
And make him toil to turn aside those blocks
Which I alone could not remove with safety.
Drusus once gone, Germanicus' three sons
Would clog my way; whose guards have too much faith   395
To be corrupted, and their mother known
Of too too unreproved a chastity
To be attempted as light Livia was.
Work then, my art, on Caesar's fears, as they
On those they fear, till all my lets be clear'd,        400
And he in ruins of his house, and hate
Of all his subjects, bury his own state;

400 lets] bets F

---

377 BUSINESS *trisyllabic.*
378 PRESENT *immediate.*
381 SECOND *support.*
384 IN BLOOD *in a mood to perpetrate cruel acts.*
385 LATE *i.e. late afternoon.*
386 EARLY *i.e. early morning.*
400 LETS *hindrances.*

When, with my peace and safety, I will rise,
By making him the public sacrifice.                              [*Exit.*]

        [*Agrippina's house. Enter*] *Satrius* [*and*] *Natta.*

405    *Satrius.* They're grown exceeding circumspect and wary.
    *Natta.* They have us in the wind. And yet Arruntius
Cannot contain himself.
    *Satrius.*            Tut, he's not yet
Looked after; there are others more desired
That are more silent.
    *Natta.*          Here he comes. Away.     [*Exeunt.*]
        [*Enter*] *Sabinus, Arruntius,* [*and*] *Cordus.*

410    *Sabinus.* How is it that these beagles haunt the house
Of Agrippina?
    *Arruntius.*    Oh, they hunt, they hunt.
There is some game here lodged, which they must rouse
To make the great ones sport.
    *Cordus.*            Did you observe
How they inveighed 'gainst Caesar?
    *Arruntius.*           Aye, baits, baits
415 For us to bite at. Would I have my flesh
Torn by the public hook, these qualified hangmen
Should be my company.         *Afer passeth by.*
    *Cordus.*        Here comes another.
    *Arruntius.* Aye, there's a man, Afer the orator!
One that hath phrases, figures, and fine flow'rs
420 To strew his rhetoric with, and doth make haste
To get him note or name by any offer
Where blood or gain be objects; steeps his words,
When he would kill, in artificial tears—

---

406 THEY . . . WIND *They scent us, as the deer scents the hunter.*
416 PUBLIC HOOK *wielded by the public hangman, to drag the bodies of executed
    criminals to the Gemonian steps, and then, three days later, to the Tiber.*

The crocodile of Tiber! Him I love;
That man is mine. He hath my heart and voice,                    425
When I would curse: he, he!
   *Sabinus.*                   Contemn the slaves;
Their present lives will be their future graves.     [*Exeunt.*]
          [*Enter*] *Silius, Agrippina, Nero,* [*and*] *Sosia.*
   *Silius.* May't please your highness not forget yourself.
I dare not, with my manners, to attempt
Your trouble farther.
   *Agrippina.*          Farewell, noble Silius.                    430
   *Silius.* Most royal princess.
   *Agrippina.*              Sosia stays with us?
   *Silius.* She is your servant, and doth owe your grace
An honest but unprofitable love.
   *Agrippina.* How can that be, when there's no gain but virtue's?
   *Silius.* You take the moral not the politic sense.                    435
I meant, as she is bold and free of speech,
Earnest to utter what her zealous thought
Travails withal, in honor of your house.
Which act, as it is simply borne in her,
Partakes of love and honesty, but may,                    440
By th'over-often and unseasoned use,
Turn to your loss and danger. For your state
Is waited on by envies, as by eyes;
And every second guest your tables take
Is a fee'd spy, t'observe who goes, who comes,                    445
What conference you have, with whom, where, when;

---

434 virtue's] virtuous F

435 POLITIC *worldly.*
438 TRAVAILS WITHAL *is pregnant with.*
439 ACT *form of behavior.* SIMPLY BORNE *carried out in simplicity of spirit.*
441 UNSEASONED *unseasonable, inopportune.*
443 WAITED . . . EYES *watched by the envious as well as the prying.*

Act II

What the discourse is, what the looks, the thoughts
Of ev'ry person there, they do extract
And make into a substance.

    *Agrippina.*                 Hear me, Silius.

450  Were all Tiberius' body stuck with eyes,
And ev'ry wall and hanging in my house
Transparent as this lawn I wear, or air;
Yea, had Sejanus both his ears as long
As to my inmost closet, I would hate

455  To whisper any thought, or change an act,
To be made Juno's rival. Virtue's forces
Show ever noblest in conspicuous courses.

    *Silius.* 'Tis great, and bravely spoken, like the spirit
Of Agrippina, yet your highness knows

460  There is nor loss nor shame in providence.
Few can, what all should do, beware enough.
You may perceive with what officious face
Satrius and Natta, Afer, and the rest
Visit your house of late, t'enquire the secrets,

465  And with what bold and privileged art they rail
Against Augusta, yea, and at Tiberius,
Tell tricks of Livia and Sejanus—all
T'excite and call your indignation on,
That they might hear it at more liberty.

    *Agrippina.* Yo'are too suspicious, Silius.

470    *Silius.*                        Pray the gods
I be so, Agrippina, but I fear
Some subtle practice. They that durst to strike

---

449 *Agrippina*] ARR. Q,F

457 CONSPICUOUS *visible, unconcealed.*
460 PROVIDENCE *foresight.*
472 PRACTICE *scheme.*

At so exampless and unblamed a life
As that of the renowned Germanicus,
Will not sit down with that exploit alone.                         475
He threatens many, that hath injured one.
   *Nero.* 'Twere best rip forth their tongues, sear out their eyes,
When next they come.
   *Sosia.*           A fit reward for spies.
                        *[Enter] Drusus Junior.*
   *Drusus.* Hear you the rumor?
   *Agrippina.*           What?
   *Drusus.*               Drusus is dying.
   *Agrippina.* Dying?
   *Nero.*       That's strange!
   *Agrippina.*               Yo' were with him, yesternight.   480
   *Drusus.* One met Eudemus the physician,
Sent for but now, who thinks he cannot live.
   *Silius.* Thinks? If't be arrived at that, he knows,
Or none.
   *Agrippina.* This's quick! What should be his disease?
   *Silius.* Poison. Poison—
   *Agrippina.*         How, Silius!
   *Nero.*               What's that?                 485
   *Silius.* Nay, nothing. There was late a certain blow
Giv'n o'the face.
   *Nero.*      Aye, to Sejanus?
   *Silius.*            True.
   *Drusus.* And what of that?
   *Silius.*            I'am glad I gave it not.
   *Nero.* But there is somewhat else?
   *Silius.*               Yes, private meetings
With a great lady, at a physician's,                               490

473 EXAMPLESS *unexampled.*
484 SHOULD BE *is reported to be.*

Act II

And a wife turned away—
   *Nero.*                    Ha!
   *Silius.*                         Toys, mere toys.
What wisdom's now i'th'streets, i'th'common mouth?
   *Drusus.* Fears, whisp'rings, tumults, noise, I know not what.
They say the Senate sit.
   *Silius.*              I'll thither, straight,
495  And see what's in the forge.
   *Agrippina.*            Good Silius, do.
Sosia and I will in.
   *Silius.*           Haste you, my lords,
To visit the sick prince. Tender your loves
And sorrows to the people. This Sejanus—
Trust my divining soul—hath plots on all.
500  No tree that stops his prospect but must fall.       [*Exeunt.*]

               *Chorus of Musicians.*

# Act III

The Senate.
[*Enter*] *Sejanus, Varro, Latiaris, Cotta, Afer, Praecones,*
[*and*] *Lictores.*

*Sejanus.* 'Tis only you must urge against him, Varro.
Nor I nor Caesar may appear therein,
Except in your defense, who are the consul,
And under color of late enmity
Between your father and his, may better do it,        5
As free from all suspicion of a practice.
Here be your notes, what points to touch at. Read;
Be cunning in them. Afer has them too.
    *Varro.* But is he summoned?
    *Sejanus.*                         No. It was debated
By Caesar and concluded as most fit        10
To take him unprepared.
    *Afer.*                         And prosecute
All under name of treason.
    *Varro.*                    I conceive.
        [*Enter Sabinus, Gallus, Lepidus, and Arruntius.*]

11 take him] him take F

___

5 YOUR . . . HIS *N.*
6 PRACTICE *plot.*
11–12 AND . . . TREASON *N.*

## Act III

*Sabinus.* Drusus being dead, Caesar will not be here.

*Gallus.* What should the business of this Senate be?

15 *Arruntius.* That can my subtle whisperers tell you. We
That are the good, dull, noble lookers-on,
Are only called to keep the marble warm.
What should we do with those deep mysteries,
Proper to these fine heads? Let them alone.
20 Our ignorance may, perchance, help us be saved
From whips and furies.

  *Gallus.*     See, see, see, their action!

  *Arruntius.* Aye, now their heads do travail; now they work!
Their faces run like shuttles; they are weaving
Some curious cobweb to catch flies.

  *Sabinus.*       Observe,
They take their places.

  *Arruntius.*  What, so low?

25   *Gallus.*         Oh, yes,
They must be seen to flatter Caesar's grief,
Though but in sitting.

  *Varro.*    Bid us silence.

  *Praeco.*       Silence!

  *Varro.* "Fathers conscript, may this our present meeting
Turn fair and fortunate to the commonwealth."

      *[Enter Silius and other senators.]*

  *Sejanus.* See, Silius enters.

  *Silius.*      Hail, grave fathers!

30   *Lictor.*          Stand.
Silius, forbear thy place.

  *Senators.*    How!

  *Praeco.*      Silius, stand forth.
The consul hath to charge thee.

17 MARBLE *i.e. the benches.*
24 CURIOUS *intricately wrought.*

84

*Lictor.*                    Room for Caesar!

*Arruntius.* Is he come too? Nay then, expect a trick.

*Sabinus.* Silius accused? Sure he will answer nobly.

               *[Enter]* Tiberius, *[attended.]*

*Tiberius.* We stand amazèd, fathers, to behold         35

This general dejection. Wherefore sit

Rome's consuls thus dissolved, as they had lost

All the remembrance both of style and place?

It not becomes. No woes are of fit weight

To make the honor of the empire stoop;        40

Though I, in my peculiar self, may meet

Just reprehension, that so suddenly,

And in so fresh a grief, would greet the Senate,

When private tongues of kinsmen and allies,

Inspired with comforts, loathly are endured,       45

The face of men not seen, and scarce the day,

To thousands that communicate our loss.

Nor can I argue these of weakness, since

They take but natural ways; yet I must seek

For stronger aids, and those fair helps draw out    50

From warm embraces of the commonwealth.

Our mother, great Augusta, 'is struck with time,

Ourself impressed with agèd characters.

Drusus is gone, his children young, and babes.

Our aims must now reflect on those that may      55

Give timely succor to these present ills,

And are our only glad-surviving hopes,

35–81 *N.*

37 DISSOLVED *discomposed.*

41 PECULIAR *individual.*

45 LOATHLY *with difficulty.*

47 COMMUNICATE *share.*

48–9 NOR . . . WAYS *Nor can I tax them with weakness, those who mourn, since they are merely obeying a natural instinct.*

## Act III

The noble issue of Germanicus,
Nero and Drusus. Might it please the consul
60 Honor them in—they both attend without—
I would present them to the Senate's care,
And raise those suns of joy that should drink up
These floods of sorrow in your drownèd eyes.
    *Arruntius.* By Jove, I am not Œdipus enough
To understand this Sphinx.
65     *Sabinus.*               The princes come.
             *[Enter] Nero [and] Drusus Junior.*
    *Tiberius.* Approach you, noble Nero, noble Drusus.
These princes, fathers, when their parent died,
I gave unto their uncle with this prayer:
That, though h'had proper issue of his own,
70 He would no less bring up and foster these
Than that self blood, and by that act confirm
Their worths to him and to posterity.
Drusus ta'en hence, I turn my prayers to you,
And, 'fore our country and our gods, beseech
75 You take and rule Augustus' nephew's sons,
Sprung of the noblest ancestors, and so
Accomplish both my duty and your own.
Nero and Drusus, these shall be to you
In place of parents, these your fathers, these,
80 And not unfitly. For you are so born
As all your good or ill's the commonwealth's.
Receive them, you strong guardians, and, blest gods,
Make all their actions answer to their bloods.
Let their great titles find increase by them,
85 Not they by titles. Set them, as in place

62 suns] springs Q   drink up] exhaust Q

---

71 SELF *same.*
85 PLACE *rank.*

86

So in example, above all the Romans;
And may they know no rivals but themselves.
Let fortune give them nothing, but attend
Upon their virtue, and that still come forth
Greater than hope, and better than their fame.                    90
Relieve me, fathers, with your general voice.
    *Senators.* "May all the gods consent to Caesar's wish,
And add to any honors that may crown
The hopeful issue of Germanicus."
    *Tiberius.* We thank you, reverend fathers, in their right.    95
    *Arruntius.* [*Aside.*] If this were true now! But the space, the
      space
Between the breast and lips—Tiberius' heart
Lies a thought farther than another man's.
    *Tiberius.* My comforts are so flowing in my joys
As, in them, all my streams of grief are lost,                   100
No less than are land waters in the sea,
Or show'rs in rivers, though their cause was such
As might have sprinkled ev'n the gods with tears.
Yet since the greater doth embrace the less,
We covetously obey.
    *Arruntius.* [*Aside.*]   Well acted, Caesar.                   105
    *Tiberius.* And now I am the happy witness made
Of your so much desired affections
To this great issue, I could wish the fates
Would here set peaceful period to my days.
However, to my labors, I entreat                                 110

86 EXAMPLE *exemplary conduct.*
92–4 MAY . . . GERMANICUS *"A form of speaking they had," explains Jonson*
    *marginally.*
104–5 YET SINCE . . . OBEY *Yet since my greater cause of tears—joy for the happy*
    *bestowal of the princes—includes the lesser cause—the death of Drusus—I*
    *yield greedily to the desire to weep.*

And beg it of this Senate, some fit ease.

    *Arruntius.* [*Aside.*] Laugh, fathers, laugh! Ha' you no spleens
        about you?

    *Tiberius.* The burden is too heavy I sustain

On my unwilling shoulders, and I pray

115 It may be taken off, and reconferred

Upon the consuls, or some other Roman,

More able and more worthy.

    *Arruntius.* [*Aside.*]        Laugh on, still.

    *Sabinus.* Why, this doth render all the rest suspected!

    *Gallus.* It poisons all.

    *Arruntius.*        Oh, d'you taste it then?

120     *Sabinus.* It takes away my faith to anything

He shall hereafter speak.

    *Arruntius.*        Aye, to pray that

Which would be to his head as hot as thunder—

'Gainst which he wears that charm—should but the court

Receive him at his word.

    *Gallus.*        Hear!

    *Tiberius.*        For myself,

125 I know my weakness, and so little covet—

Like some gone past—the weight that will oppress me,

As my ambition is the counterpoint.

    *Arruntius.* [*Aside.*] Finely maintained, good still.

    *Sejanus.*        But Rome, whose blood,

Whose nerves, whose life, whose very frame relies

130 On Caesar's strength, no less than heav'n on Atlas,

---

112 SPLEENS *traditionally, the seat of laughter.*

113–27 *N.*

119 TASTE IT *appreciate his duplicity.*

123 THAT CHARM *identified marginally by Jonson as "a wreath of laurel" worn
      superstitiously by Tiberius as protection against lightning and thunder.*

127 COUNTERPOINT *the exact reverse—i.e. total anonymity.*

Cannot admit it but with general ruin.
   *Arruntius.* [*Aside.*] Ah! Are you there, to bring him off?
   *Sejanus.*                           Let Caesar
No more, then, urge a point so contrary
To Caesar's greatness, the grieved Senate's vows,
Or Rome's necessity.
   *Gallus* [*Aside.*]    He comes about.                 135
   *Arruntius.* [*Aside.*] More nimbly than Vertumnus.
   *Tiberius.*                      For the public,
I may be drawn to show I can neglect
All private aims, though I affect my rest.
But if the Senate still command me serve,
I must be glad to practice my obedience.        140
   *Arruntius.* [*Aside.*] You must and will, sir. We do know it.
   *Senators.*                   "Caesar,
Live long and happy, great and royal Caesar!
The gods preserve thee and thy modesty,
Thy wisdom, and thy innocence."
   *Arruntius.* [*Aside.*]         Where is't?
The prayer's made before the subject.
   *Senators.*               "Guard      145
His meekness, Jove, his piety, his care,
His bounty—"
   *Arruntius.* [*Aside.*] And his subtlety, I'll put in.
Yet he'll keep that himself, without the gods.
All prayers are vain for him.
   *Tiberius.*          We will not hold
Your patience, fathers, with long answer, but     150
Shall still contend to be what you desire,
And work to satisfy so great a hope.

136 VERTUMNUS *an Etruscan god of fruits, associated with the changing year.*
138 AFFECT MY REST *value my tranquillity and peace of mind.*
142–4 CAESAR . . . INNOCENCE *"Another form," indicates Jonson marginally.*

Proceed to your affairs.

    *Arruntius.* [*Aside.*]    Now, Silius, guard thee.
The curtain's drawing. Afer advanceth.

    *Praeco.*                      Silence!

    *Afer.* Cite Caius Silius.

    *Praeco.*          Caius Silius!

155    *Silius.*                      Here.

    *Afer.* The triumph that thou hadst in Germany
For thy late victory on Sacrovir,
Thou hast enjoyed so freely, Caius Silius,
As no man it envied thee. Nor would Caesar

160 Or Rome admit that thou wert then defrauded
Of any honors thy deserts could claim
In the fair service of the commonwealth.
But now, if after all their loves and graces,
Thy actions and their courses being discovered,

165 It shall appear to Caesar and this Senate,
Thou hast defiled those glories with thy crimes—

    *Silius.* Crimes!

    *Afer.*          Patience, Silius.

    *Silius.*                 Tell thy mule of patience.
I'am a Roman. What are my crimes? Proclaim them.
Am I too rich? Too honest for the times?

170 Have I or treasure, jewels, land, or houses
That some informer gapes for? Is my strength
Too much to be admitted? Or my knowledge?
These now are crimes.

    *Afer.*           Nay, Silius, if the name

---

154 AFER *N.*
157 SACROVIR *See above, II.289–90.*
160 ADMIT *permit.*
170–1 HAVE I ∴ . FOR? *N.*

Of crime so touch thee, with what impotence
Wilt thou endure the matter to be searched?                    175
   *Silius.* I tell thee, Afer, with more scorn than fear:
Employ your mercenary tongue and art.
Where's my accuser?
   *Varro.*       Here.
   *Arruntius.* [*Aside.*]    Varro? The consul?
Is he thrust in?
   *Varro.*    'Tis I accuse thee, Silius.
Against the majesty of Rome and Caesar,                         180
I do pronounce thee here a guilty cause,
First, of beginning and occasioning,
Next, drawing out the war in Gallia,
For which thou late triumph'st; dissembling long
That Sacrovir to be an enemy                                    185
Only to make thy entertainment more,
Whilst thou and thy wife Sosia polled the province;
Wherein, with sordid-base desire of gain,
Thou hast discredited thy actions' worth
And been a traitor to the state.
   *Silius.*          Thou liest.                             190
   *Arruntius.* [*Aside.*] I thank thee, Silius, speak so still and often.
   *Varro.* If I not prove it, Caesar, but unjustly
Have called him into trial, here I bind
Myself to suffer what I claim 'gainst him,
And yield to have what I have spoke confirmed              195
By judgment of the court and all good men.
   *Silius.* Caesar, I crave to have my cause deferred

174 IMPOTENCE *lack of self-restraint.*
181–90 N.
184 TRIUMPH'ST *enjoyed a formal triumph.*
187 POLLED *fleeced.*
190 THOU LIEST N.
197–208 N.

Till this man's consulship be out.

   *Tiberius.*                 We cannot,

Nor may we grant it.

   *Silius.*            Why? Shall he design

200   My day of trial? Is he my accuser,

And must he be my judge?

   *Tiberius.*              It hath been usual

And is a right that custom hath allowed

The magistrate, to call forth private men,

And to appoint their day; which privilege

205   We may not in the consul see infringed,

By whose deep watches and industrious care

It is so labored, as the commonwealth

Receive no loss by any oblique course.

   *Silius.* Caesar, thy fraud is worse than violence.

210    *Tiberius.* Silius, mistake us not. We dare not use

The credit of the consul to thy wrong,

But only do preserve his place and power

So far as it concerns the dignity

And honor of the state.

   *Arruntius.*          Believe him, Silius.

   *Cotta.* Why, so he may, Arruntius.

215    *Arruntius.*                I say so,

And he may choose, too.

   *Tiberius.*           By the capitol

And all our gods, but that the dear republic,

Our sacred laws, and just authority

Are interested therein, I should be silent.

199 DESIGN *designate.*

204 APPOINT THEIR DAY *name the day of their trial.*

206 WATCHES *vigils.*

209 FRAUD *The custom alluded to by Tiberius apparently had reference to martial law only, and hence was inapplicable in the present situation.*

219 INTERESTED *concerned.*

*Afer*. Please' Caesar to give way unto his trial.    220
He shall have justice.

   *Silius*.            Nay, I shall have law,
Shall I not, Afer? Speak.

   *Afer*.             Would you have more?

   *Silius*. No, my well-spoken man, I would no more,
Nor less, might I enjoy it natural,
Not taught to speak unto your present ends,    225
Free from thine, his, and all your unkind handling,
Furious enforcing, most unjust presuming,
Malicious and manifold applying,
Foul wresting, and impossible construction.

   *Afer*. He raves, he raves.

   *Silius*.           Thou durst not tell me so    230
Hadst thou not Caesar's warrant. I can see
Whose power condemns me.

   *Varro*.          This betrays his spirit.
This doth enough declare him what he is.

   *Silius*. What am I? Speak.

   *Varro*.            An enemy to the state.

   *Silius*. Because I am an enemy to thee,    235
And such corrupted ministers o'the state,
That here art made a present instrument
To gratify it with thine own disgrace.

   *Sejanus*. This, to the consul, is most insolent!
And impious!

222 more] mo F

_____

224 NATURAL *unconstrained.*
226 UNKIND *unnatural.*
228 APPLYING *interpreting.*
229 CONSTRUCTION *misconstruing.*
238 DISGRACE *dishonor.*
240 IMPIOUS *because Roman magistrates performed religious as well as civil
     duties.*

240    *Silius.*        Aye, take part. Reveal yourselves.
Alas, I scent not your confed'racies,
Your plots, and combinations? I not know
Minion Sejanus hates me, and that all
This boast of law, and law, is but a form,
245 A net of Vulcan's filing, a mere engine
To take that life by a pretext of justice
Which you pursue in malice? I want brain
Or nostril to persuade me that your ends
And purposes are made to what they are,
250 Before my answer? O, you equal gods,
Whose justice not a world of wolf-turned men
Shall make me to accuse, howe'er provoked,
Have I for this so oft engaged myself?
Stood in the heat and fervor of a fight,
255 When Phoebus sooner hath forsook the day
Than I the field, against the blue-eyed Gauls,
And crispèd Germans? When our Roman eagles
Have fanned the fire with their laboring wings,
And no blow dealt that left not death behind it?
260 When I have charged alone into the troops
Of curled Sicambrians, routed them, and came

---

240 *Silius*] SEJ. Q
252 provoked] provoke Q,F

---

245 NET . . . FILING *a snare of the sort in which Vulcan trapped his wife, Venus, in adultery with Mars.* ENGINE *trap.*
248 NOSTRIL *acuteness.*
248–50 YOUR ENDS . . . ANSWER *you have reached your conclusions, for your own purposes, before you have heard my testimony.*
250 EQUAL *just.*
257 CRISPÈD *curly-haired.*
261 CURLED SICAMBRIANS *mentioned by Martial as among the exotic foreigners who flocked to Rome to see the spectacles.*

Not off with backward ensigns of a slave,
But forward marks, wounds on my breast and face,
Were meant to thee, O Caesar, and thy Rome?
And have I this return? Did I, for this,                          265
Perform so noble and so brave defeat
On Sacrovir? O Jove, let it become me
To boast my deeds, when he whom they concern
Shall thus forget them!
   *Afer.*           Silius, Silius,
These are the common customs of thy blood,                        270
When it is high with wine, as now with rage.
This well agrees with that intemperate vaunt
Thou lately mad'st at Agrippina's table,
That when all other of the troops were prone
To fall into rebellion, only yours                                275
Remained in their obedience. You were he
That saved the empire, which had then been lost,
Had but your legions there rebelled or mutined.
Your virtue met and fronted every peril.
You gave to Caesar and to Rome their surety.                      280
Their name, their strength, their spirit, and their state,
Their being was a donative from you.

275 yours] thine Q
276 You were] Thou wert Q
277 saved] sav'dst Q
278 your] thy Q
279 Your] Thy Q
280 You gave] Thou gav'st Q
282 you] thee Q

---

262–3 NOT OFF . . . FACE *not wounded in the back, fleeing like a coward, but in
      front, like a fighter.*
264 MEANT TO THEE *suffered in your behalf.*
272–8, 288–91, 305–8 N.
275 YOURS N.
278 MUTINED *mutinied.*
282 DONATIVE *gift.*

*Arruntius. [Aside.]* Well worded, and most like an orator.
*Tiberius.* Is this true, Silius?
*Silius.*                    Save thy question, Caesar.
285   Thy spy of famous credit hath affirmed it.
*Arruntius. [Aside.]* Excellent Roman!
*Sabinus. [Aside.]*                    He doth answer stoutly.
*Sejanus.* If this be so, there needs no farther cause
Of crime against him.
*Varro.*              What can more impeach
The royal dignity and state of Caesar,
290   Than to be urgèd with a benefit
He cannot pay?
*Cotta.*        In this, all Caesar's fortune
Is made unequal to the courtesy.
*Latiaris.* His means are clean destroyed, that should requite.
*Gallus.* Nothing is great enough for Silius' merit.
*Arruntius. [Aside.]* Gallus on that side too?
295   *Silius.*                              Come, do not hunt
And labor so about for circumstance,
To make him guilty whom you have foredoomed.
Take shorter ways; I'll meet your purposes.
The words were mine, and more I now will say:
300   Since I have done thee that great service, Caesar,
Thou still hast feared me, and in place of grace
Returned me hatred. So soon all best turns,
With doubtful princes, turn deep injuries
In estimation, when they greater rise

295 on] o' Q
303 With doubtful princes, turn deep] With Princes, do convert to Q

287–8 CAUSE OF CRIME *ground of accusation.*
301 STILL *always.*
303 DOUBTFUL *suspicious N.*
304 ESTIMATION *valuation.*

Than can be answered. Benefits, with you,                    305
Are of no longer pleasure than you can
With ease restore them. That transcended once,
Your studies are not how to thank, but kill.
It is your nature to have all men slaves
To you, but you acknowledging to none.                        310
The means that makes your greatness must not come
In mention of it. If it do, it takes
So much away, you think, and that which helped
Shall soonest perish, if it stand in eye
Where it may front, or but upbraid the high.                  315
   *Cotta.* Suffer him speak no more.
   *Varro.*              Note but his spirit.
   *Afer.* This shows him in the rest.
   *Latiaris.*           Let him be censured.
   *Sejanus.* He'hath spoke enough to prove him Caesar's foe.
   *Cotta.* His thoughts look through his words.
   *Sejanus.*              A censure.
   *Silius.*                  Stay,
Stay, most officious Senate, I shall straight                 320
Delude thy fury. Silius hath not placed
His guards within him, against fortune's spite,
So weakly but he can escape your gripe
That are but hands of Fortune. She herself,

---

311 makes] make Q

---

305 ANSWERED *repaid.*
306–7 ARE OF . . . THEM *please you only so long as you can easily requite them.*
307 THAT *that situation.*
314 STAND IN EYE *be visible.*
315 FRONT *confront.*
317 SHOWS *reveals.* CENSURED *judged.*
319 LOOK *are visible.*
324 ARE *is.* SHE *Fortune.*

97

325 When virtue doth oppose, must lose her threats.
All that can happen in humanity,
The frown of Caesar, proud Sejanus' hatred,
Base Varro's spleen, and Afer's bloodying tongue,
The Senate's servile flattery, and these
330 Mustered to kill I'am fortified against,
And can look down upon; they are beneath me.
It is not life whereof I stand enamored,
Nor shall my end make me accuse my fate.
The coward and the valiant man must fall;
335 Only the cause and manner how, discerns them,
Which then are gladdest when they cost us dearest.
Romans, if any here be in this Senate,
Would know to mock Tiberius' tyranny,
Look upon Silius, and so learn to die.                    [*Stabs himself.*]
    *Varro.* Oh, desperate act!
340     *Arruntius* [*Aside.*]        An honorable hand!
    *Tiberius.* Look, is he dead?
    *Sabinus.* [*Aside.*]        'Twas nobly struck, and home.
    *Arruntius.* [*Aside.*] My thought did prompt him to it. Farewell,
    Silius!
Be famous ever for thy great example.
    *Tiberius.* We are not pleased in this sad accident,
345 That thus hath stallèd and abused our mercy,
Intended to preserve thee, noble Roman,
And to prevent thy hopes.
    *Arruntius.* [*Aside.*]        Excellent wolf!

335 DISCERNS *differentiates.*
336 WHICH . . . DEAREST *that form of death is most welcome which most keenly
    puts us to the test.*
338 KNOW *know how.*
345 STALLÈD *brought to a halt, forestalled.*
347 PREVENT *anticipate.*

Now he is full, he howls.
 *Sejanus.*     Caesar doth wrong
His dignity and safety, thus to mourn
The deserved end of so professed a traitor       350
And doth, by this his lenity, instruct
Others as factious to the like offense.
 *Tiberius.* The confiscation merely of his state
Had been enough.
 *Arruntius.* [*Aside.*] Oh, that was gaped for then?
 *Varro.* Remove the body.
 *Sejanus.*     Let citation     355
Go out for Sosia.
 *Gallus.*  Let her be proscribed.
And for the goods, I think it fit that half
Go to the treasure, half unto the children.
 *Lepidus.* With leave of Caesar, I would think that fourth
Part, which the law doth cast on the informers,    360
Should be enough, the rest go to the children;
Wherein the prince shall show humanity
And bounty, not to force them by their want—
Which in their parents' trespass they deserved—
To take ill courses.
 *Tiberius.*  It shall please us.
 *Arruntius.* [*Aside.*]     Aye,    365
Out of necessity. This Lepidus
Is grave and honest, and I have observed
A moderation still in all his censures.
 *Sabinus.* And bending to the better—
[*Enter*] *Satrius* [*and*] *Natta,* [*with Cremutius*] *Cordus,* [*guarded.*]
        Stay, who's this?

360 Part, which] The which Q

355–69 N.
368 CENSURES *judgments.*

Act III

370 Cremutius Cordus? What? Is he brought in?
    *Arruntius.* More blood unto the banquet? Noble Cordus,
I wish thee good. Be as thy writings, free
And honest.
    *Tiberius.* What is he?
    *Sejanus.*            For th'annals, Caesar.
    *Praeco.* Cremutius Cordus!
    *Cordus.*              Here.
    *Praeco.*                 Satrius Secundus,
375 Pinnarius Natta, you are his accusers.
    *Arruntius.* Two of Sejanus' bloodhounds, whom he breeds
With human flesh, to bay at citizens.
    *Afer.* Stand forth before the Senate and confront him.
    *Satrius.* I do accuse thee here, Cremutius Cordus,
380 To be a man factious and dangerous,
A sower of sedition in the state,
A turbulent and discontented spirit;
Which I will prove from thine own writings here,
The annals thou hast published, where thou bit'st
385 The present age, and with a viper's tooth,
Being a member of it, dar'st that ill
Which never yet degenerous bastard did
Upon his parent.
    *Natta.*       To this I subscribe,
And, forth a world of more particulars,
390 Instance in only one: comparing men
And times, thou praisest Brutus, and affirm'st

384 hast] last Q

372 FREE *noble.*
379–406 N.
387 DEGENEROUS *degenerate.*
389 FORTH *from out of.*

That Cassius was the last of all the Romans.
    *Cotta.* How! What are we then?
    *Varro.*                     What is Caesar? Nothing?
    *Afer.* My lords, this strikes at every Roman's private,
In whom reigns gentry and estate of spirit,                           395
To have a Brutus brought in parallel,
A parricide, an enemy of his country,
Ranked and preferred to any real worth
That Rome now holds. This is most strangely invective,
Most full of spite, and insolent upbraiding.                          400
Nor is't the time alone is here disprized,
But the whole man of time, yea, Caesar's self
Brought in disvalue, and he aimed at most
By oblique glance of his licentious pen.
Caesar, if Cassius were the last of Romans,                           405
Thou hast no name.
    *Tiberius.*           Let's hear him answer. Silence.
    *Cordus.* So innocent I am of fact, my lords,
As but my words are argued. Yet those words
Not reaching either prince, or prince's parent,
The which your law of treason comprehends.                            410
Brutus and Cassius I am charged t'have praised,
Whose deeds, when many more besides myself
Have writ, not one hath mentioned without honor.

---

394 *Afer*] ARR. Q

394 PRIVATE *private self, personal honor.*
395 GENTRY *nobility.* ESTATE *dignity.*
397 PARRICIDE *traitor.*
401 DISPRIZED *belittled.*
402 WHOLE . . . TIME *the greatest man of the present day.*
407–60 N.
407 FACT *deed.*
409 REACHING *extending to.* PARENT *kinsman.*

Act III

Great Titus Livius, great for eloquence
415  And faith amongst us, in his history,
With so great praises Pompey did extol
As oft Augustus called him a Pompeian—
Yet this not hurt their friendship. In his book
He often names Scipio, Afranius,
420  Yea, the same Cassius, and this Brutus too,
As worthiest men, not thieves and parricides,
Which notes upon their fames are now imposed.
Asinius Pollio's writings quite throughout
Give them a noble memory. So Messalla
425  Renowned his general Cassius. Yet both these
Lived with Augustus full of wealth and honors.
To Cicero's book, where Cato was heaved up
Equal with heav'n, what else did Caesar answer,
Being then dictator, but with a penned oration,
430  As if before the judges? Do but see
Antonius' letters; read but Brutus' pleadings,
What vile reproach they hold against Augustus—
False, I confess, but with much bitterness.

414 TITUS LIVIUS *Roman patriotic historian of the reign of Augustus.*
419 SCIPIO *Metellus Scipio, Pompey's father-in-law and cohort in the campaign against Caesar.* AFRANIUS *a member of the same faction, Pompey's emissary in Spain.*
422 NOTES *black marks.*
423 ASINIUS POLLIO *an enemy of Augustus during the Civil Wars, and later a historian of them.*
424 MESSALLA *a supporter of Brutus and Cassius at the battle of Philippi, afterward an orator and historian.*
427–8 CICERO'S BOOK . . . ANSWER *A tract by Cicero praising Cato was answered by one from Caesar attacking him.*
427 HEAVED UP *exalted N.*
431 ANTONIUS' LETTERS *A few are quoted by Suetonius* (Augustus). BRUTUS' PLEADINGS *Nothing is known of these.*

The epigrams of Bibaculus and Catullus
Are read, full stuffed with spite of both the Caesars.                    435
Yet deified Julius, and no less Augustus,
Both bore them, and contemned them—I not know
Promptly to speak it, whether done with more
Temper or wisdom—for such obloquies
If they despisèd be, they die suppressed;                                 440
But if with rage acknowledged, they are confessed.
The Greeks I slip, whose license not alone,
But also lust did scape unpunishèd.
Or where some one, by chance, exception took,
He words with words revenged. But in my work.                            445
What could be aimed more free, or farther off
From the time's scandal, than to write of those
Whom death from grace or hatred had exempted?
Did I, with Brutus and with Cassius,
Armed and possessed of the Philippi fields,                              450
Incense the people in the civil cause,
With dangerous speeches? Or do they, being slain
Seventy years since, as by their images—
Which not the conqueror hath defaced—appears,
Retain that guilty memory with writers?                                  455
Posterity pays every man his honor.
Nor shall there want, though I condemnèd am,

434 EPIGRAMS . . . CATULLUS *Some anti-Caesarian lampoons of Catullus
    survive; those of Bibaculus, a friend of Catullus, do not.*
438 PROMPTLY *readily.*
439 TEMPER *equanimity.*
440–1 SUPPRESSED . . . CONFESSED *N.*
442 SLIP *pass over.*
446 AIMED MORE FREE *more innocent in purpose.*
453 IMAGES *statues.*
455 RETAIN . . . WRITERS? [*Are they*] *remembered only for their crimes?*

That will not only Cassius well approve,
And of great Brutus' honor mindful be,
460 But that will also mention make of me.
   *Arruntius.* Freely and nobly spoken.
   *Sabinus.*                       With good temper.
I like him, that he is not moved with passion.
   *Arruntius.* He puts 'em to their whisper.
   *Tiberius.*                   Take him hence.
We shall determine of him at next sitting.
                      *[Exeunt guards with Cordus.]*
465    *Cotta.* Meantime, give order that his books be burnt,
To the aediles.
   *Sejanus.*     You have well advised.
   *Afer.* It fits not such licentious things should live
T'upbraid the age.
   *Arruntius. [Aside.]* If th'age were good, they might.
   *Latiaris.* Let 'em be burnt.
   *Gallus.*               All sought and burnt today.
470    *Praeco.* The court is up. Lictors, resume the fasces.
       *[Exeunt all but]* Arruntius, Sabinus, *[and]* Lepidus.
   *Arruntius.* Let 'em be burnt! Oh, how ridiculous
Appears the Senate's brainless diligence,
Who think they can, with present power, extinguish
The memory of all succeeding times!
475    *Sabinus.* 'Tis true, when contrary, the punishment
Of wit doth make th'authority increase.
Nor do they aught, that use this cruelty
Of interdiction, and this rage of burning,

466 AEDILES *municipal officers.*
470 LICTORS *officials who bore the fasces and executed judgment on offenders.*
471–80 N.
476 WIT *literary achievement.*
477 THAT USE *those who practice.*

But purchase to themselves rebuke and shame,
And to the writers an eternal name.                                    480
   *Lepidus.* It is an argument the times are sore,
When virtue cannot safely be advanced,
Nor vice reproved.
   *Arruntius.*       Aye, noble Lepidus.
Augustus well foresaw what we should suffer
Under Tiberius, when he did pronounce                                   485
The Roman race most wretched, that should live
Between so slow jaws, and so long a bruising.     [*Exeunt.*]

   [*The imperial palace. Enter*] *Tiberius* [*and*] *Sejanus.*
   *Tiberius.* This business hath succeeded well, Sejanus,
And quite removed all jealousy of practice
'Gainst Agrippina and our nephews. Now                                 490
We must bethink us how to plant our engines
For th'other pair, Sabinus and Arruntius.
And Gallus too: howe'er he flatter us,
His heart we know.
   *Sejanus.*       Give it some respite, Caesar.
Time shall mature, and bring to perfect crown                          495
What we, with so good vultures, have begun.
Sabinus shall be next.
   *Tiberius.*       Rather Arruntius.
   *Sejanus.* By any means, preserve him. His frank tongue
Being lent the reins, will take away all thought
Of malice in your course against the rest.                             500

482 ADVANCED *honored.*
489 JEALOUSY OF PRACTICE *suspicion of a plot.*
491 PLANT OUR ENGINES *lay our snares.*
496 WITH . . . VULTURES *so auspiciously (referring to divination based on flights
    of birds).*

We must keep him to stalk with.
 *Tiberius.*        Dearest head,
To thy most fortunate design I yield it.
 *Sejanus.* Sir—I'have been so long trained up in grace,
First with your father, great Augustus, since
505 With your most happy bounties so familiar,
As I not sooner would commit my hopes
Or wishes to the gods, than to your ears.
Nor have I ever yet been covetous
Of overbright and dazzling honors; rather
510 To watch and travail in great Caesar's safety,
With the most common soldier.
 *Tiberius.*       'Tis confessed.
 *Sejanus.* The only gain, and which I count most fair
Of all my fortunes, is that mighty Caesar
Hath thought me worthy his alliance. Hence
Begin my hopes.
 *Tiberius.*    H'mh?
515 *Sejanus.*       I have heard, Augustus,
In the bestowing of his daughter, thought
But even of gentlemen of Rome. If so—
I know not how to hope so great a favor—
But if a husband should be sought for Livia,
520 And I be had in mind, as Caesar's friend,
I would but use the glory of the kindred.
It should not make me slothful or less caring
For Caesar's state. It were enough to me
505 With ... familiar] To ... inur'd Q

---

501 TO STALK WITH *as a stalking horse, to help trap the others.*
503–76 N.
509 RATHER *preferring rather.*
514 WORTHY HIS ALLIANCE N.
517 GENTLEMEN OF ROME *equestrian knights, usually private citizens.*
521 I ... KINDRED *I would profit only from the prestige of the alliance.*

It did confirm and strengthen my weak house
Against the now unequal opposition                                    525
Of Agrippina. And for dear regard
Unto my children, this I wish. Myself
Have no ambition farther than to end
My days in service of so dear a master.

    *Tiberius.* We cannot but commend thy piety,        530
Most loved Sejanus, in acknowledging
Those bounties, which we, faintly, such remember—
But to thy suit. The rest of mortal men,
In all their drifts and counsels, pursue profit.
Princes alone are of a different sort,                                535
Directing their main actions still to fame.
We therefore will take time to think and answer.
For Livia, she can best herself resolve
If she will marry after Drusus, or
Continue in the family. Besides,                                     540
She hath a mother and a grandam yet,
Whose nearer counsels she may guide her by—
But I will simply deal. That enmity
Thou fear'st in Agrippina would burn more,
If Livia's marriage should, as 'twere in parts,                      545
Divide th'imperial house. An emulation
Between the women might break forth, and discord
Ruin the sons and nephews on both hands.
What if it cause some present difference?
Thou art not safe, Sejanus, if thou prove it.                        550

529  master] Prince Q
530  piety] pity Q

---

530 ff. *N.*
530 PIETY *dutiful affection.*
543 SIMPLY *straightforwardly.*
549 PRESENT DIFFERENCE *immediate quarrel.*
550 PROVE *try.*

## Act III

Canst thou believe that Livia, first the wife
To Caius Caesar, then my Drusus, now
Will be contented to grow old with thee,
Born but a private gentleman of Rome?
555 And raise thee with her loss, if not her shame?
Or say that I should wish it, canst thou think
The Senate, or the people, who have seen
Her brother, father, and our ancestors,
In highest place of empire, will endure it?
560 The state thou hold'st already, is in talk.
Men murmur at thy greatness, and the nobles
Stick not in public to upbraid thy climbing
Above our father's favors, or thy scale,
And dare accuse me, from their hate to thee.
565 Be wise, dear friend. We would not hide these things
For friendship's dear respect. Nor will we stand
Adverse to thine or Livia's designments.
What we had purposed to thee, in our thought,
And with what near degrees of love to bind thee,
570 And make thee equal to us, for the present
We will forbear to speak. Only thus much
Believe, our loved Sejanus, we not know
That height in blood or honor, which thy virtue
And mind to us may not aspire with merit.
575 And this we'll publish on all watched occasion
The Senate or the people shall present.

551 first the] who was Q
552 my] to Q

555 AND . . . SHAME N.
560 STATE *high rank, greatness.*
560–4 N.
563 SCALE *rank, degree.*
575 ON . . . OCCASION *at every opportunity we spy.*

*Sejanus.* I am restored, and to my sense again,
Which I had lost in this so blinding suit.
Caesar hath taught me better to refuse
Than I knew how to ask. How pleaseth Caesar                    580
T'embrace my late advice for leaving Rome?
    *Tiberius.* We are resolved.
    *Sejanus.* [*Gives him a paper.*] Here are some motives more,
Which I have thought on since, may more confirm.
    *Tiberius.* Careful Sejanus! We will straight peruse them.
Go forward in our main design and prosper.          [*Exit.*]     585
    *Sejanus.* If those but take, I shall. Dull, heavy Caesar!
Would'st thou tell me thy favors were made crimes?
And that my fortunes were esteemed thy faults?
That thou, for me, wert hated? And not think
I would with wingèd haste prevent that change,                  590
When thou might'st win all to thyself again
By forfeiture of me? Did those fond words
Fly swifter from thy lips than this my brain,
This sparkling forge, created me an armor
T'encounter chance, and thee? Well, read my charms,            595
And may they lay that hold upon thy senses
As thou hadst snuffed up hemlock, or ta'en down
The juice of poppy and of mandrakes. Sleep,
Voluptuous Caesar, and security
Seize on thy stupid powers, and leave them dead                600

584 CAREFUL *conscientious, painstaking.*
586 THOSE *the "motives" he has just handed Caesar.* TAKE *persuade.*
590–2 PREVENT . . . ME *anticipate and forestall any attempt of yours to regain your former power by sacrificing me.*
592 FOND *foolish.*
595 CHARMS *the paper given Tiberius, with reasons why he should leave Rome.*
599 SECURITY *carelessness.*

Act III

To public cares, awake but to thy lusts.
The strength of which makes thy libidinous soul
Itch to leave Rome; and I have thrust it on,
With blaming of the city business,
605   The multitude of suits, the confluence
Of suitors, then their importunacies,
The manifold distractions he must suffer,
Besides ill rumors, envies, and reproaches—
All which, a quiet and retired life,
610   Larded with ease and pleasure, did avoid;
And yet, for any weighty'and great affair,
The fittest place to give the soundest counsels.
By this shall I remove him both from thought
And knowledge of his own most dear affairs,
615   Draw all dispatches through my private hands,
Know his designments, and pursue mine own,
Make mine own strengths by giving suits and places,
Conferring dignities and offices;
And these that hate me now, wanting access
620   To him, will make their envy none, or less.
For when they see me arbiter of all,
They must observe, or else with Caesar fall.          [*Exit.*]
              [*Re-enter*] *Tiberius.*

    *Tiberius.* To marry Livia! Will no less, Sejanus,
Content thy aims? No lower object? Well!
625   Thou know'st how thou art wrought into our trust,
Woven in our design, and think'st we must
Now use thee, whatsoe'er thy projects are.
'Tis true. But yet with caution and fit care.

603–20 N.
610 DID *would.*
614 DEAR *intimate, important.*
622 OBSERVE *pay homage.*

And, now we better think—Who's there, within?

[*Enter Servus.*]

*Servus.* Caesar?

*Tiberius.*       To leave our journey off were sin    630
'Gainst our decreed delights, and would appear
Doubt, or—what less becomes a prince—low fear.
Yet doubt hath law, and fears have their excuse,
Where princes' states plead necessary use,
As ours doth now—more in Sejanus' pride    635
Than all fell Agrippina's hates beside.
Those are the dreadful enemies we raise
With favors, and make dangerous with praise.
The injured by us may have will alike,
But 'tis the favorite hath the power to strike.    640
And fury ever boils more high and strong,
Heat' with ambition, than revenge of wrong.
'Tis then a part of supreme skill, to grace
No man too much, but hold a certain space
Between th'ascender's rise and thine own flat,    645
Lest, when all rounds be reached, his aim be that.
'Tis thought—Is Macro in the palace? See.
If not, go seek him, to come to us.    [*Exit Servus.*]
                    He
Must be the organ we must work by now,
Though none less apt for trust. Need doth allow    650
What choice would not. I'have heard that aconite,

---

637 Those] They Q

---

636 FELL *ruthless.*
637–46 N.
642 HEAT *heated.*
645 FLAT *level.*
646 ROUNDS *rungs (of a ladder).*
651 ACONITE *herbal poison.*

## Act III

Being timely taken, hath a healing might
Against the scorpion's stroke. The proof we'll give,
That, while two poisons wrestle, we may live.
655 He hath a spirit too working to be used
But to th'encounter of his like. Excused
Are wiser sov'reigns then, that raise one ill
Against another, and both safely kill.
The prince that feeds great natures, they will sway him;
660 Who nourisheth a lion must obey him.
     *[Re-enter Servus with] Macro.*
Macro, we sent for you.
  *Macro.*    I heard so, Caesar.
  *Tiberius.* Leave us awhile.     *[Exit Servus.]*
       When you shall know, good Macro,
The causes of our sending, and the ends,
You then will hearken nearer, and be pleased
665 You stand so high both in our choice and trust.
  *Macro.* The humblest place in Caesar's choice or trust
May make glad Macro proud—without ambition,
Save to do Caesar service.
  *Tiberius.*    Leave our courtings.
We are in purpose, Macro, to depart
670 The city for a time, and see Campania—
Not for our pleasures, but to dedicate
A pair of temples, one to Jupiter
At Capua, th'other at Nola, to Augustus,
In which great work, perhaps our stay will be

---

653 THE PROOF . . . GIVE *We'll put it to the test.*
654 THAT *in the hope that.*
655 WORKING *active, energetic.*
656 BUT . . . LIKE *except pitted against someone of his own kind—i.e. Sejanus.*
668 OUR COURTINGS *courting us.*

Beyond our will produced. Now, since we are       675
Not ignorant what danger may be born
Out of our shortest absence, in a state
So subject unto envy, and embroiled
With hate and faction, we have thought on thee,
Amongst a field of Romans, worthiest Macro,       680
To be our eye and ear, to keep strict watch
On Agrippina, Nero, Drusus—aye,
And on Sejanus—not that we distrust
His loyalty or do repent one grace
Of all that heap we have conferred on him.       685
For that were to disparage our election,
And call that judgment now in doubt, which then
Seemed as unquestioned as an oracle—
But greatness hath his cankers. Worms and moths
Breed out of too fit matter in the things       690
Which after they consume, transferring quite
The substance of their makers int' themselves.
Macro is sharp, and apprehends. Besides,
I know him subtle, close, wise, and well read
In man and his large nature. He hath studied       695
Affections, passions; knows their springs, their ends;
Which way, and whether they will work. 'Tis proof
Enough of his great merit that we trust him.
Then, to a point—because our conference

690 fit matter] much humor Q

---

675 PRODUCED *prolonged.*
686 ELECTION *choice.*
690 TOO FIT MATTER *matter too apt for its own destruction, too well adapted to be the prey of worms and moths, which, by eating it (691), assimilate its properties into themselves (691–2).*
693 APPREHENDS *understands.*
699 TO A POINT *to come to the point.*

## Act III

700 Cannot be long without suspicion—
Here, Macro, we assign thee, both to spy,
Inform, and chastise. Think, and use thy means,
Thy ministers, what, where, on whom thou wilt.
Explore, plot, practice. All thou dost in this
705 Shall be as if the Senate or the laws
Had giv'n it privilege, and thou thence styled
The savior both of Caesar and of Rome.
We will not take thy answer but in act,
Whereto, as thou proceed'st, we hope to hear
710 By trusted messengers. If't be enquired
Wherefore we called you, say you have in charge
To see our chariots ready and our horse.
Be still our loved, and (shortly) honored Macro.          [*Exit.*]
   *Macro.* I will not ask why Caesar bids do this,
715 But joy that he bids me. It is the bliss
Of courts to be employed, no matter how.
A prince's power makes all his actions virtue.
We, whom he works by, are dumb instruments,
To do, but not enquire. His great intents
720 Are to be served, not searched. Yet, as that bow
Is most in hand whose owner best doth know
T'affect his aims, so let that statesman hope
Most use, most price, can hit his prince's scope.
Nor must he look at what or whom to strike,
725 But loose at all; each mark must be alike.

---

707 savior] savier F

---

714–49 N.
720–3 YET . . . SCOPE *Yet as that bow is most effectively wielded by the archer*
    *who best knows how to aim, so that prince's servant may expect most*
    *employment, most reward, who best can fall in with his master's purposes.*
725 LOOSE *let fly (continuing the figure from archery).* MARK *butt, target.* ALIKE
    *equal.*

Were it to plot against the fame, the life
Of one with whom I twinned; remove a wife
From my warm side, as loved as is the air;
Practice away each parent; draw mine heir
In compass, though but one; work all my kin                    730
To swift perdition; leave no untrained engine
For friendship, or for innocence; nay, make
The gods all guilty: I would undertake
This, being imposed me, both with gain and ease.
The way to rise is to obey and please.                         735
He that will thrive in state, he must neglect
The trodden paths that truth and right respect,
And prove new, wilder ways; for virtue, there,
Is not that narrow thing she is elsewhere.
Men's fortune there is virtue; reason, their will;             740
Their license, law; and their observance, skill.
Occasion is their foil; conscience, their stain;
Profit, their luster; and what else is, vain.
If then it be the lust of Caesar's power
T'have raised Sejanus up, and in an hour                       745
O'erturn him, tumbling down from height of all,
We are his ready engine, and his fall

728 AS LOVED . . . AIR *because air is essential to life.*
729 PRACTICE AWAY *undo by plotting.*
730 IN COMPASS *within the network of my intrigues.* THOUGH BUT ONE *though
    I had only a single heir.*
731 NO UNTRAINED ENGINE *no trap unset.*
736 STATE *the political world.*
738 PROVE *try out.*
741 OBSERVANCE *obsequious respect.*
742 FOIL *what sets them off, adorns them.*
744 LUST *inclination.*
747 ENGINE *instrument.*

Act III

May be our rise. It is no uncouth thing
To see fresh buildings from old ruins spring.          [*Exit.*]

*Chorus of Musicians.*

748 UNCOUTH *unknown, unprecedented.*

# Act IV

[*Agrippina's house. Enter*] *Gallus* [*and*] *Agrippina.*
*Gallus.* You must have patience, royal Agrippina.
  *Agrippina.* I must have vengeance first, and that were nectar
Unto my famished spirits. O, my fortune,
Let it be sudden thou prepar'st against me.
Strike all my powers of understanding blind,                    5
And ignorant of destiny to come.
Let me not fear, that cannot hope.
  *Gallus.*                    Dear princess,
These tyrannies on yourself are worse than Caesar's.
  *Agrippina.* Is this the happiness of being born great?
Still to be aimed at? Still to be suspected?                    10
To live the subject of all jealousies?
At the least, color made, if not the ground
To every painted danger? Who would not
Choose once to fall, than thus to hang forever?
  *Gallus.* You might be safe, if you would—
  *Agrippina.*                    What, my Gallus?    15
Be lewd Sejanus' strumpet? Or the bawd

10 STILL *forever.*
12–13 COLOR . . . DANGER *made the pretext* ("*color*"), *if not the basis* ("*ground*"
      —*i.e. background), of every feigned* ("*painted*") *danger.*
14 ONCE *once for all.*

117

Act IV

To Caesar's lusts, he now is gone to practice?
Not these are safe, where nothing is. Yourself,
While thus you stand but by me, are not safe.
20 Was Silius safe? Or the good Sosia safe?
Or was my niece, dear Claudia Pulchra, safe?
Or innocent Furnius? They that latest have,
By being made guilty, added reputation
To Afer's eloquence? O foolish friends,
25 Could not so fresh example warn your loves,
But you must buy my favors with that loss
Unto yourselves, and when you might perceive
That Caesar's cause of raging must forsake him,
Before his will? Away, good Gallus, leave me.
30 Here to be seen, is danger; to speak, treason;
To do me least observance is called faction.
You are unhappy'in me, and I in all.
Where are my sons, Nero and Drusus? We
Are they be shot at. Let us fall apart,
35 Not in our ruins sepulcher our friends.
Or shall we do some action like offense,
To mock their studies, that would make us faulty,
And frustrate practice by preventing it?
The danger's like, for what they can contrive
40 They will make good. No innocence is safe,
When power contests. Nor can they trespass more,

25 SO *such a.*
28–9 THAT . . . WILL *that Caesar's rage will not cease until its cause, I myself, am
removed.*
31 OBSERVANCE *respectful courtesy.*
34 APART *separately, by ourselves.*
36–8 OR SHALL . . . IT? *Or shall we commit some act resembling the offence we
are charged with, to defy their attempts to make criminals of us, and baffle
their plot by anticipating it?*
39 LIKE *equal.*

118

Whose only being was all crime before.

        [*Enter Nero, Drusus, and Caligula.*]

  *Nero.* You hear Sejanus is come back from Caesar?

  *Gallus.* No. How? Disgraced?

  *Drusus.*                More gracèd now than ever.

  *Gallus.* By what mischance?

  *Caligula.*              A fortune like enough     45

Once to be bad.

  *Drusus.*      But turned too good to both.

  *Gallus.* What was't?

  *Nero.*             Tiberius sitting at his meat,

In a farmhouse they call Spelunca, sited

By the seaside, among the Fundane hills,

Within a natural cave, part of the grot     50

About the entry fell, and overwhelmed

Some of the waiters; others ran away.

Only Sejanus, with his knees, hands, face,

O'erhanging Caesar, did oppose himself

To the remaining ruins, and was found     55

In that so laboring posture by the soldiers

That came to succor him. With which adventure

He hath so fixed himself in Caesar's trust

As thunder cannot move him, and is come

With all the height of Caesar's praise, to Rome.     60

  *Agrippina.* And power to turn those ruins all on us,

And bury whole posterities beneath them.

Nero and Drusus and Caligula,

Your places are the next, and therefore most

In their offense. Think on your birth and blood;     65

42 WHOSE . . . BEFORE *whose mere existence was already an unpardonable crime.*
47–60 N.
52 WAITERS *attendants.*
65 THEIR *Sejanus' and Tiberius'.*

Act IV

Awake your spirits; meet their violence.
'Tis princely when a tyrant doth oppose,
And is a fortune sent to exercise
Your virtue, as the wind doth try strong trees,
70  Who by vexation grow more sound and firm.
After your father's fall, and uncle's fate,
What can you hope, but all the change of stroke
That force or sleight can give? Then stand upright,
And though you do not act, yet suffer nobly.
75  Be worthy of my womb, and take strong cheer.
What we do know will come, we should not fear.     [*Exeunt.*]
                    [*The street. Enter*] *Macro.*
    *Macro.* Returned so soon? Renewed in trust and grace?
Is Caesar then so weak? Or hath the place
But wrought this alteration with the air,
80  And he, on next remove, will all repair?
Macro, thou art engaged, and what before
Was public, now must be thy private, more.
The weal of Caesar fitness did imply,
But thine own fate confers necessity
85  On thy employment; and the thoughts borne nearest
Unto ourselves move swiftest still, and dearest.

70 VEXATION *shaking, agitation.*
72 CHANGE OF STROKE *diversity of blows.*
78 THE PLACE *where Tiberius has been on vacation.*
80 ON NEXT REMOVE *at his next stop.*
81 ENGAGED *committed.*
81–2 WHAT . . . MORE *what started as a matter of public duty has now become even more a matter of personal survival.*
83 WEAL *welfare.* FITNESS DID IMPLY *argued the desirability of executing his commands.*
85–6 BORNE . . . OURSELVES *most deeply affecting our own welfare.*
86 MOVE . . . DEAREST *always lead most quickly to action, and the deepest involvement in action.*

If he recover, thou art lost. Yea, all
The weight of preparation to his fall
Will turn on thee and crush thee. Therefore, strike
Before he settle, to prevent the like                                    90
Upon thyself. He doth his vantage know,
That makes it home, and gives the foremost blow.          [*Exit.*]

  [*An upper room of Agrippina's house. Enter*] Latiaris, Rufus,
         [*and*] Opsius.
 *Latiaris.* It is a service great Sejanus will
See well requited, and accept of nobly.
Here place yourselves, between the roof and ceiling,                      95
And when I bring him to his words of danger,
Reveal yourselves, and take him.
 *Rufus.*       Is he come?
 *Latiaris.* I'll now go fetch him.      [*Exit.*]
 *Opsius.*      With good speed. I long
To merit from the state, in such an action.
 *Rufus.* I hope it will obtain the consulship                        100
For one of us.
 *Opsius.*  We cannot think of less,
To bring in one so dangerous as Sabinus.
 *Rufus.* He was a follower of Germanicus,
And still is an observer of his wife
And children, though they be declined in grace—                          105
A daily visitant, keeps them company
In private and in public, and is noted

93 great] Lord Q

---

87 HE *Sejanus.*
92 MAKES IT HOME *exploits it to the full.* FOREMOST *first.*
93–232 N.
95 BETWEEN . . . CEILING N.
104 OBSERVER *follower, visitant.*
105 DECLINED IN GRACE *out of favor.*

To be the only client of the house.
Pray Jove he will be free to Latiaris.

110     *Opsius.* He's allied to him, and doth trust him well.
    *Rufus.* And he'll requite his trust?
    *Opsius.*                      To do an office
So grateful to the state, I know no man
But would strain nearer bands than kindred—
    *Rufus.*                      List,
I hear them come.
    *Opsius.*         Shift to our holes with silence.   [*They retire.*]
    [*Re-enter*] Latiaris [*with*] Sabinus.

115     *Latiaris.* It is a noble constancy you show
To this afflicted house, that not like others,
The friends of season, you do follow fortune,
And in the winter of their fate, forsake
The place whose glories warmed you. You are just,
120 And worthy such a princely patron's love,
As was the world's renowned Germanicus,
Whose ample merit when I call to thought,
And see his wife and issue objects made
To so much envy, jealousy, and hate,
125 It makes me ready to accuse the gods
Of negligence, as men of tyranny.
    *Sabinus.* They must be patient, so must we.
    *Latiaris.*                     O Jove!
What will become of us, or of the times,
When to be high or noble are made crimes?
130 When land and treasure are most dangerous faults?

109 FREE *open, candid.*
110 ALLIED TO HIM *N.*
111 REQUITE *i.e. betray.*
117 FRIENDS OF SEASON *fair weather friends.*
127 THEY . . . WE *N.*

   *Sabinus.* Nay, when our table, yea our bed, assaults
Our peace and safety? When our writings are,
By any envious instruments that dare
Apply them to the guilty, made to speak
What they will have, to fit their tyrannous wreak?         135
When ignorance is scarcely innocence,
And knowledge made a capital offense?
When not so much but the bare empty shade
Of liberty is reft us? And we made
The prey to greedy vultures and vile spies,         140
That first transfix us with their murdering eyes?
   *Latiaris.* Methinks the genius of the Roman race
Should not be so extinct, but that bright flame
Of liberty might be revived again—
Which no good man but with his life should lose—         145
And we not sit like spent and patient fools,
Still puffing in the dark at one poor coal,
Held on by hope, till the last spark is out.
The cause is public, and the honor, name,
The immortality of every soul         150
That is not bastard or a slave in Rome,
Therein concerned. Whereto, if men would change
The wearied arm, and for the weighty shield
So long sustained, employ the ready sword,
We might have some assurance of our vows.         155
This ass's fortitude doth tire us all.
It must be active valor must redeem
Our loss, or none. The rock and our hard steel

---

154 ready] facile Q

135 WREAK *vengeance.*
138 NOT . . . BUT *even.*
140–1 SPIES . . . EYES *N.*

Should meet t'enforce those glorious fires again
160   Whose splendor cheered the world and heat gave life
No less than doth the sun's.

    *Sabinus.*                'Twere better stay
In lasting darkness and despair of day.
No ill should force the subject undertake
Against the sovereign, more than hell should make
165   The gods do wrong. A good man should and must
Sit rather down with loss than rise unjust.
Though, when the Romans first did yield themselves
To one man's power, they did not mean their lives,
Their fortunes, and their liberties should be
170   His absolute spoil, as purchased by the sword.

    *Latiaris.* Why, we are worse, if to be slaves, and bond
To Caesar's slave, be such, the proud Sejanus—
He that is all, does all, gives Caesar leave
To hide his ulcerous and anointed face,
175   With his bald crown at Rhodes, while he here stalks
Upon the heads of Romans and their princes,
Familiarly to empire.

    *Sabinus.*          Now you touch
A point indeed, wherein he shows his art,
As well as power.

    *Latiaris.*        And villainy in both.
180   Do you observe where Livia lodges? How
Drusus came dead? What men have been cut off?

    *Sabinus.* Yes, those are things removed. I nearer looked

---

166 SIT . . . UNJUST *submit patiently to deprivation, rather than rebel.*
167–70 THOUGH . . . SWORD *a significant qualification to the* jus divinum
       *sentiments just expressed.*
175 RHODES *N.*
177 FAMILIARLY *unceremoniously.* EMPIRE *the imperial throne.*
182 REMOVED *remote in time.*

Into his later practice, where he stands
Declared a master in his mystery.
First, ere Tiberius went, he wrought his fear                    185
To think that Agrippina sought his death.
Then put those doubts in her; sent her oft word,
Under the show of friendship, to beware
Of Caesar, for he laid to poison her;
Drave them to frowns, to mutual jealousies,                     190
Which now in visible hatred are burst out.
Since, he hath had his hired instruments
To work on Nero, and to heave him up;
To tell him Caesar's old; that all the people,
Yea, all the army have their eyes on him;                       195
That both do long to have him undertake
Something of worth, to give the world a hope;
Bids him to court their grace. The easy youth,
Perhaps, gives ear, which straight he writes to Caesar,
And with this comment: "See yon dangerous boy.                  200
Note but the practice of the mother, there.
She's tying him, for purposes at hand,
With men of sword." Here's Caesar put in fright
'Gainst son and mother. Yet he leaves not thus.
The second brother, Drusus, a fierce nature,                    205
And fitter for his snares, because ambitious
And full of envy, him he clasps and hugs,
Poisons with praise, tells him what hearts he wears,

182–3 I NEARER . . . PRACTICE *I was referring particularly to his more recent
            intrigues.*
184 MYSTERY *trade.*
185 WROUGHT *brought about.*
189 FOR HE LAID *because he was plotting.*
190 DRAVE *drove.* JEALOUSIES *suspicions.*
193 HEAVE . . . UP *incite him.*
202 TYING *allying.*

Act IV

How bright he stands in popular expectance;
210  That Rome doth suffer with him in the wrong
His mother does him by preferring Nero.
Thus sets he them asunder, each 'gainst other,
Projects the course that serves him to condemn,
Keeps in opinion of a friend to all,
And all drives on to ruin.
215  *Latiaris.*                    Caesar sleeps,
And nods at this?
        *Sabinus.*        Would he might ever sleep,
Bogged in his filthy lusts.
                        [*Opsius and Rufus rush in.*]
        *Opsius.*                    Treason to Caesar!
*Rufus.* Lay hands upon the traitor, Latiaris,
Or take the name thyself.
        *Latiaris.*                    I am for Caesar.
        *Sabinus.* Am I then catched?
220  *Rufus.*                        How think you, sir? You are.
*Sabinus.* Spies of this head! So white, so full of years!
Well, my most reverend monsters, you may live
To see youselves thus snared.
        *Opsius.*                        Away with him!
*Latiaris.* Hale him away.
        *Rufus.*                        To be a spy for traitors
Is honorable vigilance.
225  *Sabinus.*                    You do well,
My most officious instruments of state,
Men of all uses. Drag me hence, away.
The year is well begun, and I fall fit
To be an off'ring to Sejanus. Go.

209 POPULAR EXPECTANCE *the expectations of the people.*
228–9 THE YEAR . . . SEJANUS *N.*

*Opsius.* Cover him with his garments, hide his face.                     230
   *Sabinus.* It shall not need. Forbear your rude assault,
The fault's not shameful villainy makes a fault.          [*Exeunt.*]

     [*The street. Enter*] *Macro* [*and*] *Caligula.*

   *Macro.* Sir, but observe how thick your dangers meet
In his clear drifts! Your mother and your brothers
Now cited to the Senate! Their friend Gallus                     235
Feasted today by Caesar, since committed!
Sabinus here we met, hurried to fetters!
The senators all struck with fear and silence,
Save those whose hopes depend not on good means,
But force their private prey from public spoil.                     240
And you must know, if here you stay, your state
Is sure to be the subject of his hate,
As now the object.
   *Caligula.*      What would you advise me?
   *Macro.* To go for Capreae presently, and there
Give up yourself entirely to your uncle.                     245
Tell Caesar (since your mother is accused
To fly for succors to Augustus' statue,
And to the army, with your brethren) you
Have rather chose to place your aids in him,
Than live suspected, or in hourly fear                     250
To be thrust out by bold Sejanus' plots.
Which you shall confidently urge to be
Most full of peril to the state and Caesar,

---

230 COVER . . . FACE *part of the customary formula whereby criminals were
     condemned to death.*
234 CLEAR DRIFTS *obvious designs.*
239 GOOD MEANS *private fortunes.*
241 STATE *status, i.e. as a member of the royal family.*
247 TO FLY . . . TO *of seeking refuge at.*

As being laid to his peculiar ends,
255 And not to be let run with common safety.
All which, upon the second, I'll make plain,
So both shall love and trust with Caesar gain.
    *Caligula.* Away then, let's prepare us for our journey.
                              *[Exeunt.]*
               *[Enter] Arruntius.*
    *Arruntius.* Still dost thou suffer, heav'n? Will no flame,
260 No heat of sin make thy just wrath to boil
In thy distempered bosom, and o'erflow
The pitchy blazes of impiety
Kindled beneath thy throne? Still canst thou sleep,
Patient, while vice doth make an antic face
265 At thy dread power, and blow dust and smoke
Into thy nostrils? Jove, will nothing wake thee?
Must vile Sejanus pull thee by the beard
Ere thou wilt open thy black-lidded eye,
And look him dead? Well, snore on, dreaming gods,
270 And let this last of that proud giant race
Heave mountain upon mountain 'gainst your state.
Be good unto me, Fortune, and you powers
Whom I, expostulating, have profaned.
I see—what's equal with a prodigy—
275 A great, a noble Roman, and an honest,
Live an old man!
               *[Enter Lepidus.]*

257 So] And Q

---

254 LAID . . . ENDS *designed to further his private aims.*
255 LET RUN *allowed free rein.*
256 UPON THE SECOND *in your support.*
264 ANTIC FACE *grimace.*
269 LOOK HIM DEAD *kill him with a look.*
273 EXPOSTULATING *complaining to.*

Oh, Marcus Lepidus,
When is our turn to bleed? Thyself and I,
Without our boast, are almost all the few
Left to be honest in these impious times.

*Lepidus.* What we are left to be, we will be, Lucius,      280
Though tyranny did stare as wide as death,
To fright us from it.

*Arruntius.*     'T hath so, on Sabinus.

*Lepidus.* I saw him now drawn from the Gemonies,
And, what increased the direness of the fact,
His faithful dog, upbraiding all us Romans,      285
Never forsook the corpse, but, seeing it thrown
Into the stream, leaped in, and drowned with it.

*Arruntius.* O act to be envied him of us men!
We are the next the hook lays hold on, Marcus.
What are thy arts—good patriot, teach them me—      290
That have preserved thy hairs to this white dye,
And kept so reverend and so dear a head
Safe on his comely shoulders?

*Lepidus.*     Arts, Arruntius?
None but the plain and passive fortitude
To suffer and be silent; never stretch      295
These arms against the torrent; live at home,
With my own thoughts and innocence about me,
Not tempting the wolf's jaws: these are my arts.

*Arruntius.* I would begin to study 'em, if I thought

283 GEMONIES *stairs on the Aventine hill to which the bodies of executed criminals were dragged by the hangman, and from which they were then flung into the Tiber.*
284 FACT *deed.*
285–7 N.
288 OF *by.*
289 HOOK *executioner's hook.*
293–8 N.

300 They would secure me. May I pray to Jove
In secret, and be safe? Aye, or aloud?
With open wishes? So I do not mention
Tiberius or Sejanus? Yes, I must
If I speak out. 'Tis hard, that. May I think,
305 And not be racked? What danger is't to dream,
Talk in one's sleep, or cough? Who knows the law?
May'I shake my head without a comment? Say
It rains, or it holds up, and not be thrown
Upon the Gemonies? These now are things
310 Whereon men's fortune, yea, their fate depends.
Nothing hath privilege 'gainst the violent ear.
No place, no day, no hour we see is free—
Not our religious and most sacred times—
From some one kind of cruelty. All matter,
315 Nay, all occasion pleaseth. Madmen's rage,
The idleness of drunkards, women's nothing,
Jesters' simplicity—all, all is good
That can be catched at. Nor is now th'event
Of any person, or for any crime,
320 To be expected, for 'tis always one:
Death, with some little difference of place
Or time—what's this? Prince Nero? Guarded?

> [*Enter Laco and Nero with guards.*]
> *Laco.* On, lictors, keep your way. My lords, forbear.

300 SECURE ME *make me safe.*
305 RACKED *tortured on the rack, to reveal his thoughts.*
307 WITHOUT A COMMENT *without some spy claiming it to be treason.*
311 VIOLENT *which violates, i.e. maliciously distorts, everything it hears.*
314–5 ALL MATTER . . . PLEASETH *Any pretext, any occasion, will serve to
  launch the charge of treason.*
316 NOTHING *empty chitchat.*
318 CATCHED AT *seized upon.* EVENT *outcome.*
320 EXPECTED *doubtfully awaited.*

On pain of Caesar's wrath, no man attempt
Speech with the prisoner.

   *Nero.*                Noble friends, be safe.        325
To lose yourselves for words were as vain hazard
As unto me small comfort. Fare you well.
Would all Rome's suff'rings in my fate did dwell.

   *Laco.* Lictors, away.

   *Lepidus.*             Where goes he, Laco?

   *Laco.*                             Sir,
He's banished into Pontia, by the Senate.        330

   *Arruntius.* Do I see? And hear? And feel? May I trust sense?
Or doth my fancy form it?

   *Lepidus.*                 Where's his brother?

   *Laco.* Drusus is prisoner in the palace.

   *Arruntius.*                Ha!
I smell it now; 'tis rank. Where's Agrippina?

   *Laco.* The princess is confined to Pandataria.        335

   *Arruntius.* Bolts, Vulcan; bolts, for Jove! Phoebus, thy bow;
Stern Mars, thy sword; and blue-eyed maid, thy spear;
Thy club, Alcides—all the armory
Of heaven is too little!—Ha! To guard
The gods, I meant. Fine, rare dispatch! This same        340
Was swiftly borne! Confined? Imprisoned? Banished?
Most tripartite! The cause, sir?

   *Laco.*                    Treason.

   *Arruntius.*                     Oh?
The complement of all accusings! That
Will hit, when all else fails.

   *Lepidus.*             This turn is strange!
345   But yesterday, the people would not hear

330, 335 PONTIA, PANDATARIA *islands in the Tyrrhenian sea near Naples.*
337 BLUE-EYED MAID *Pallas Athena.*
338 ALCIDES *Hercules.*

Act IV

Far less objected, but cried, Caesar's letters
Were false, and forged; that all these plots were malice;
And that the ruin of the prince's house
Was practiced 'gainst his knowledge. Where are now
350   Their voices, now that they behold his heirs
Locked up, disgraced, led into exile?
    *Arruntius.*                           Hushed,
Drowned in their bellies. Wild Sejanus' breath
Hath, like a whirlwind, scattered that poor dust
With this rude blast.            *He turns to Laco and the rest.*
                We'll talk no treason, sir,
355   If that be it you stand for. Fare you well.
We have no need of horseleeches. Good spy,
Now you are spied, begone.
                    *[Exeunt Laco, Nero, and guards.]*
    *Lepidus.*               I fear you wrong him.
He has the voice to be an honest Roman.
    *Arruntius.* And trusted to this office? Lepidus,
360   I'd sooner trust Greek Sinon than a man
Our state employs. He's gone, and being gone,
I dare tell you, whom I dare better trust,
That our night-eyed Tiberius doth not see
His minion's drifts. Or, if he do, he's not
365   So arrant subtle as we fools do take him,
To breed a mongrel up in his own house,
With his own blood, and, if the good gods please,
At his own throat flesh him to take a leap.
368 flesh] train Q

348 PRINCE'S *Germanicus'.*
360 GREEK SINON *who persuaded the Trojans to accept the wooden horse, hence a
      byword for a smooth-tongued villain.*
363 NIGHT-EYED *lynx-eyed.*
365 TAKE *suppose.*
368 FLESH *encourage with the taste of blood.*

I do not beg it, heav'n, but if the fates
Grant it these eyes, they must not wink.
  *Lepidus.*                 They must        370
Not see it, Lucius.
  *Arruntius.*    Who should let 'em?
  *Lepidus.*                  Zeal,
And duty, with the thought he is our prince.
  *Arruntius.* He is our monster, forfeited to vice
So far, as no racked virtue can redeem him.
His loathèd person fouler than all crimes,         375
An emp'ror only in his lusts. Retired
From all regard of his own fame, or Rome's,
Into an obscure island, where he lives,
Acting his tragedies with a comic face,
Amidst his rout of Chaldees; spending hours,     380
Days, weeks, and months, in the unkind abuse
Of grave astrology to the bane of men;
Casting the scope of men's nativities,
And having found aught worthy in their fortune,
Kill, or precipitate them in the sea,          385
And boast he can mock fate. Nay, muse not. These
Are far from ends of evil, scarce degrees.
He hath his slaughterhouse at Capreae,
Where he doth study murder as an art,

370 WINK *shut, i.e. flinch from beholding it.*
371 LET *hinder.*
374 RACKED *however wrung from him.*
379 COMIC FACE *comic mask, as used on the public stage.*
380–6 N.
380 CHALDEES *astrologers.*
381 UNKIND *unnatural.*
387 ENDS *limits, extremes.* DEGREES *intermediary stages.*

390 And they are dearest in his grace that can
Devise the deepest tortures. Thither, too,
He hath his boys and beauteous girls ta'en up
Out of our noblest houses, the best formed,
Best nurtured, and most modest. What's their good
395 Serves to provoke his bad. Some are allured;
Some threatened; others, by their friends detained,
Are ravished hence like captives, and in sight
Of their most grievèd parents, dealt away
Unto his spintries, sellaries, and slaves,
400 Masters of strange and new commented lusts,
For which wise nature hath not left a name.
To this—what most strikes us, and bleeding Rome—
He is, with all his craft, become the ward
To his own vassal, a stale catamite,
405 Whom he, upon our low and suffering necks,
Hath raised from excrement to side the gods,
And have his proper sacrifice in Rome;
Which Jove beholds, and yet will sooner rive
A senseless oak with thunder than his trunk.

      *[Re-enter] Laco [with] Pomponius [and] Minutius.*

410    *Laco.* These letters make men doubtful what t'expect,
Whether his coming, or his death.

   *Pomponius.*                   Troth, both.
And which comes soonest, thank the gods for.

391–401 N.
394–5 N.
399 SPINTRIES, SELLARIES *male prostitutes.*
400 NEW COMMENTED *newly invented.*
404 CATAMITE *boy kept for unnatural purposes.*
406 SIDE *match.*
407 PROPER *own.*
409 HIS *Sejanus'.*
410–514 N.

*Arruntius.*                                    List!
Their talk is Caesar. I would hear all voices.
        [*Arruntius and Lepidus stand aside.*]
    *Minutius.* One day he's well, and will return to Rome.
The next day sick, and knows not when to hope it.                415
    *Laco.* True, and today, one of Sejanus' friends
Honored by special writ, and on the morrow
Another punished—
    *Pomponius.*        By more special writ.
    *Minutius.* This man receives his praises of Sejanus;
A second, but slight mention; a third, none;                    420
A fourth, rebukes. And thus he leaves the Senate
Divided and suspended, all uncertain.
    *Laco.* These forkèd tricks, I understand 'em not.
Would he would tell us whom he loves or hates,
That we might follow, without fear or doubt.                    425
    *Arruntius.* [*Aside.*] Good heliotrope! Is this your honest man?
Let him be yours so still. He is my knave.
    *Pomponius.* I cannot tell; Sejanus still goes on,
And mounts, we see. New statues are advanced,
Fresh leaves of titles, large inscriptions read,                430
His fortune sworn by, himself new gone out
Caesar's colleague in the fifth consulship.
More altars smoke to him than all the gods.
What would we more?
    *Arruntius.* [*Aside.*]        That the dear smoke would choke him.
That would I more.

414 *Minutius*] MAR. Q
435 That . . . Arruntius] *Not in* Q

426 HELIOTROPE *alluding to that flower's habit, from which it derives its name, of
        turning so as always to face the sun.*
430 LEAVES *sheets.*
431 GONE *entered as.*

Act IV

435     *Lepidus.* [*Aside.*]    Peace, good Arruntius.
    *Laco.* But there are letters come, they say, ev'n now,
Which do forbid that last.
    *Minutius.*               Do you hear so?
    *Laco.*                               Yes.
    *Pomponius.* By Pollux, that's the worst.
    *Arruntius.* [*Aside.*]                 By Hercules, best!
    *Minutius.* I did not like the sign, when Regulus,
440 Whom all we know no friend unto Sejanus,
Did, by Tiberius' so precise command,
Succeed a fellow in the consulship.
It boded somewhat.
    *Pomponius.*       Not a mote. His partner,
Fulcinius Trio, is his own, and sure.
Here comes Terentius.

                   [*Enter Terentius.*]
445                    He can give us more.
                       *They whisper with Terentius.*
    *Lepidus.* I'll ne'er believe but Caesar hath some scent
Of bold Sejanus' footing. These cross-points
Of varying letters and opposing consuls,
Mingling his honors and his punishments,
450 Feigning now ill, now well, raising Sejanus
And then depressing him, as now of late
In all reports we have it, cannot be
Empty of practice. 'Tis Tiberius' art.
For, having found his favorite grown too great,

---

438 Pollux] Castor Q   Hercules] Pollux Q *N.*
449 Mingling] Mixing Q

---

438 POLLUX . . . HERCULES *N.*
443 SOMEWHAT *something.*
444 HIS *Sejanus'*. SURE *of certain loyalty.*
453 EMPTY OF PRACTICE *without significance as strategy.* ART *artfulness.*

And, with his greatness, strong; that all the soldiers                455
Are, with their leaders, made at his devotion;
That almost all the Senate are his creatures,
Or hold on him their main dependences,
Either for benefit, or hope, or fear;
And that himself hath lost much of his own,                          460
By parting unto him, and by th'increase
Of his rank lusts and rages, quite disarmed
Himself of love, or other public means
To dare an open contestation—
His subtlety hath chose this doubling line                           465
To hold him even in; not so to fear him,
As wholly put him out, and yet give check
Unto his farther boldness. In meantime,
By his employments, makes him odious
Unto the staggering rout, whose aid, in fine,                        470
He hopes to use, as sure—who, when they sway,
Bear down, o'erturn all objects in their way.
   *Arruntius.* You may be a Lynceus, Lepidus, yet I
See no such cause but that a politic tyrant,
Who can so well disguise it, should have ta'en                       475
A nearer way: feigned honest, and come home

456 MADE . . . DEVOTION *wholly at his disposal.*
458 HOLD . . . DEPENDENCES *are more dependent on him than anyone else.*
461 PARTING UNTO *sharing with.*
465 DOUBLING *ambiguous, deceitful.*
466 HOLD . . . IN *keep him in check.* FEAR *frighten.*
467 PUT HIM OUT *disconcert him.*
469 BY HIS EMPLOYMENTS *by employing him as he does.*
470 STAGGERING ROUT *unstable mob.* IN FINE *at last.*
471 SURE *dependable for his purpose.* WHO *the rout.*
473 LYNCEUS *proverbially sharp-sighted Argonaut.*
474 NO SUCH . . . THAT *no reason why not.* POLITIC *crafty.*
476 NEARER *more direct.*

Act IV

To cut his throat by law.

    *Lepidus.*                Aye, but his fear
Would ne'er be masked, all-be his vices were.

    *Pomponius.* His lordship then is still in grace?

    *Terentius.*                    Assure you,
480  Never in more, either of grace or power.

    *Pomponius.* The gods are wise and just.

    *Arruntius.* [*Aside.*]        The fiends they are,
To suffer thee belie 'em!

    *Terentius.*       I have here
His last and present letters, where he writes him
"The partner of his cares," and "his Sejanus"—

485    *Laco.* But is that true, it is prohibited
To sacrifice unto him?

    *Terentius.*      Some such thing
Caesar makes scruple of, but forbids it not,
No more than to himself; says he could wish
It were forborne to all.

    *Laco.*        Is it no other?
490    *Terentius.* No other, on my trust. For your more surety,
Here is that letter too.

    *Arruntius.* [*Aside.*]   How easily
Do wretched men believe what they would have!
Looks this like plot?

    *Lepidus.* [*Aside.*] Noble Arruntius, stay.

    *Laco.* He names him here without his titles.

    *Lepidus.* [*Aside.*]            Note.
495    *Arruntius.* [*Aside.*] Yes, and come off your notable fool. I will.

    *Laco.* No other than Sejanus.

    *Pomponius.*         That's but haste

478 ALL-BE *although.*
495 COME . . . FOOL *show myself an egregious ass.*

138

In him that writes. Here he gives large amends.

    *Minutius.* And with his own hand written?

    *Pomponius.*                       Yes.

    *Laco.*                           Indeed?

    *Terentius.* Believe it, gentlemen, Sejanus' breast

Never received more full contentments in,           500

Than at this present.

    *Pomponius.*       Takes he well th'escape

Of young Caligula with Macro?

    *Terentius.*             Faith,

At the first air, it somewhat troubled him.

    *Lepidus.* [*Aside.*] Observe you?

    *Arruntius.* [*Aside.*]       Nothing. Riddles. Till I see

Sejanus struck, no sound thereof strikes me.       505

                    [*Exeunt Arruntius and Lepidus.*]

    *Pomponius.* I like it not. I muse h'would not attempt

Somewhat against him in the consulship,

Seeing the people 'gin to favor him.

    *Terentius.* He doth repent it now, but h'has employed

Pagonianus after him; and he holds           510

That correspondence there, with all that are

Near about Caesar, as no thought can pass

Without his knowledge thence, in act to front him.

    *Pomponius.* I gratulate the news.

    *Laco.*                But how comes Macro

So'in trust and favor with Caligula?           515

---

498 *Minutius*] MAR. Q,F
503 troubled] mated Q
514 *Laco*] MAC. Q,F

---

506 H' *Sejanus.*
507, 8 HIM *Caligula.*
511 CORRESPONDENCE *close communication.*
514 GRATULATE *welcome.*

Act IV

    *Pomponius.* Oh, sir, he has a wife, and the young prince
An appetite. He can look up, and spy
Flies in the roof when there are fleas i'bed,
And hath a learnèd nose to'assure his sleeps.
520 Who, to be favored of the rising sun,
Would not lend little of his waning moon?
'Tis the saf'st ambition. Noble Terentius!
    *Terentius.* The night grows fast upon us. At your service.

                                        *[Exeunt.]*

*Chorus of Musicians.*

<hr>

516 WIFE *Jonson here tampers with historical sequence. The affair between Caligula and Macro's wife took place some years later.*

140

# Act V

[*Sejanus' house. Enter*] *Sejanus.*

*Sejanus.* Swell, swell, my joys, and faint not to declare
Yourselves as ample as your causes are.
I did not live till now, this my first hour
Wherein I see my thoughts reached by my power.
But this, and gripe my wishes. Great and high,                  5
The world knows only two, that's Rome and I.
My roof receives me not; 'tis air I tread;
And at each step, I feel my'advancèd head
Knock out a star in heav'n! Reared to this height,
All my desires seem modest, poor and slight,                    10
That did before sound impudent. 'Tis place,
Not blood, discerns the noble and the base.
Is there not something more than to be Caesar?
Must we rest there? It irks t'have come so far,
To be so near a stay. Caligula,                                 15
Would thou stood'st stiff, and many in our way!
Winds lose their strength when they do empty fly,
Unmet of woods or buildings; great fires die,

5 BUT . . . WISHES *This last obstacle removed, I need only reach out and seize
what I desire.*
11 PLACE *rank.*
12 DISCERNS *distinguishes.*

Act V

That want their matter to withstand them. So
20 It is our grief, and will be'our loss, to know
Our power shall want opposites, unless
The gods, by mixing in the cause, would bless
Our fortune with their conquest. That were worth
Sejanus' strife, durst fates but bring it forth.

                *[Enter] Terentius.*

  *Terentius.* Safety to great Sejanus!
25   *Sejanus.*                 Now, Terentius?
  *Terentius.* Hears not my lord the wonder?
  *Sejanus.*                 Speak it. No.
  *Terentius.* I meet it violent in the people's mouths,
Who run in routs to Pompey's theater
To view your statue; which, they say, sends forth
30 A smoke as from a furnace, black and dreadful.
  *Sejanus.* Some traitor hath put fire in. You, go see.
And let the head be taken off, to look
What 'tis—*[Exit Servus.]* Some slave hath practiced an imposture,
To stir the people.

        *[Re-enter Servus with] Satrius, [and] Natta.*
        —How now? Why return you?
35   *Satrius.* The head, my lord, already is ta'en off.
I saw it; and, at op'ning, there leaped out
A great and monstrous serpent!
  *Sejanus.*            Monstrous? Why?
Had it a beard and horns? No heart? A tongue
Forkèd as flattery? Looked it of the hue
40 To such as live in great men's bosoms? Was
The spirit of it Macro's?

21 OPPOSITES *antagonists.*
23 THEIR CONQUEST *our conquest of them.*
25–93 N.
28 ROUTS *hordes.*

142

*Natta.*                    May it please
The most divine Sejanus, in my days—
And by his sacred fortune I affirm it—
I have not seen a more extended, grown,
Foul, spotted, venomous, ugly—
    *Sejanus.*                    Oh, the fates!                    45
What a wild muster's here of attributes,
T'express a worm, a snake!
    *Terentius.*                    But how that should
Come there, my lord!
    *Sejanus.*                    What! And you too, Terentius?
I think you mean to make't a prodigy
In your reporting.
    *Terentius.*          Can the wise Sejanus                    50
Think heav'n hath meant it less?
    *Sejanus.*                    Oh, superstition!
Why then, the falling of our bed, that brake
This morning, burdened with the populous weight
Of our expecting clients, to salute us;
Or running of the cat betwixt our legs,                    55
As we set forth unto the Capitol,
Were prodigies.
    *Terentius.*          I think them ominous,
And would they had not happened. As, today,
The fate of some your servants; who, declining
Their way, not able, for the throng, to follow,                    60
Slipped down the Gemonies and brake their necks.
Besides, in taking your last augury,
No prosperous bird appeared, but croaking ravens

---

59 declining] diverting Q

54 EXPECTING *waiting.*
59 SOME *some of.* DECLINING *turning aside from.*

Act V

Flagged up and down, and from the sacrifice
65 Flew to the prison, where they sat all night,
Beating the air with their obstreperous beaks.
I dare not counsel, but I could entreat
That great Sejanus would attempt the gods
Once more with sacrifice.

  *Sejanus.*     What excellent fools
70 Religion makes of men! Believes Terentius,
If these were dangers, as I shame to think them,
The gods could change the certain course of fate?
Or, if they could, they would, now in a moment,
For a beef's fat, or less, be bribed t'invert
75 Those long decrees? Then think the gods, like flies,
Are to be taken with the steam of flesh
Or blood diffused about their altars. Think
Their power as cheap as I esteem it small.
Of all the throng that fill th'Olympian hall,
80 And without pity lade poor Atlas' back,
I know not that one deity, but Fortune,
To whom I would throw up in begging smoke
One grain of incense, or whose ear I'd buy
With thus much oil. Her I indeed adore,
85 And keep her grateful image in my house,
Sometimes belonging to a Roman king,
But now called mine, as by the better style.
To her I care not if, for satisfying
Your scrupulous fancies, I go offer. Bid
90 Our priest prepare us honey, milk, and poppy,

64 FLAGGED *flew unsteadily.*
69 EXCELLENT *surpassing.*
85 GRATEFUL *pleasing.*
86 BELONGING . . . KING *The statue belonged previously to Servius Tullius.*

144

His masculine odors and night vestments. Say
Our rites are instant, which performed, you'll see
How vain and worthy laughter your fears be.        [*Exeunt.*]
            [*Enter*] *Cotta* [*and*] *Pomponius.*
   *Cotta.* Pomponius! Whither in such speed?
   *Pomponius.*                            I go
To give my lord Sejanus notice—
   *Cotta.*                         What?                        95
   *Pomponius.* Of Macro.
   *Cotta.*              Is he come?
   *Pomponius.*                        Entered but now
The house of Regulus.
   *Cotta.*              The opposite consul!
   *Pomponius.* Some half-hour since.
   *Cotta.*                            And by night too! Stay, sir.
I'll bear you company.
   *Pomponius.*         Along, then—                 [*Exeunt.*]

      [*Regulus's house. Enter*] *Macro, Regulus,* [*and attendant.*]
   *Macro.* 'Tis Caesar's will to have a frequent Senate,       100
And therefore must your edict lay deep mulct
On such as shall be absent.
   *Regulus.*               So it doth.
Bear it my fellow consul to adscribe.
   *Macro.* And tell him it must early be proclaimed.
The place, Apollo's temple.                [*Exit attendant.*]
   *Regulus.*              That's remembered.                   105

103 adscribe] ascribe Q
_____

91 MASCULINE ODORS *i.e. the best kind of frankincense.*
92 INSTANT *to be performed without delay.*
97 OPPOSITE *opposing.*
100 FREQUENT SENATE *full muster of the Senate.*
101 LAY DEEP MULCT *levy severe fines.*
103 ADSCRIBE *subscribe.*

Act V

    *Macro.* And at what hour.

    *Regulus.*                   Yes.

    *Macro.*                         You do forget
To send one for the provost of the watch?

    *Regulus.* I have not. Here he comes.

                      *[Enter Laco.]*

    *Macro.*                   Gracinus Laco,
You are a friend most welcome. By and by
110 I'll speak with you. *[To Regulus.]* You must procure this list
Of the praetorian cohorts, with the names
Of the centurions, and their tribunes.

    *Regulus.*                   Aye.

    *Macro.* I bring you letters and a health from Caesar.

    *Laco.* Sir, both come well.

    *Macro. [To Regulus.]*     And hear you? With your note
115 Which are the eminent men, and most of action.

    *Regulus.* That shall be done you too.

    *Macro.*                   Most worthy Laco.
Caesar salutes you. *The consul goes out.* Consul! Death and furies!
Gone now? The argument will please you, sir.
Ho, Regulus! The anger of the gods
120 Follow his diligent legs, and overtake 'em
In likeness of the gout. *[The consul] returns.* Oh, good my lord,
We lacked you present. I would pray you send
Another to Fulcinius Trio straight,
To tell him you will come and speak with him—
125 The matter we'll devise—to stay him there,
While I, with Laco, do survey the watch.

                         *[The consul] goes out again.*
What are your strengths, Gracinus?

120 his] your Q

---

111 PRAETORIAN COHORTS *companies of the guard.*
117–70 *N.*

*Laco.*                                    Seven cohorts.

*Macro.* You see what Caesar writes, and—gone again?
H'has sure a vein of mercury in his feet.
Know you what store of the praetorian soldiers                    130
Sejanus holds about him, for his guard?

*Laco.* I cannot the just number, but I think
Three centuries.

*Macro.*            Three? Good.

*Laco.*                                    At most, not four.

*Macro.* And who be those centurions?

*Laco.*                                        That the consul
Can best deliver you.

*Macro.*                    When he's away?                        135
Spite on his nimble industry. Gracinus,
You find what place you hold there in the trust
Of royal Caesar?

*Laco.*            Aye, and I am—

*Macro.*                              Sir,
The honors there proposed are but beginnings
Of his great favors.

*Laco.*                They are more—

*Macro.*                                    I heard him            140
When he did study what to add—

*Laco.*                                    My life,
And all I hold—

*Macro.*            You were his own first choice,
Which doth confirm as much as you can speak;
And will, if we succeed, make more—Your guards
Are seven cohorts, you say?

---

130 Know] Knew Q,F

---

132 CANNOT *do not know*. JUST *exact*.
133 CENTURIES *hundreds*.

  *Laco.*         Yes.

145   *Macro.*        Those we must
Hold still in readiness, and undischarged.

  *Laco.* I understand so much. But how it can—

  *Macro.* Be done without suspicion, you'll object?

        [*Re-enter Regulus.*]

  *Regulus.* What's that?

  *Laco.*       The keeping of the watch in arms
When morning comes.

150   *Macro.*      The Senate shall be met, and set
So early in the temple, as all mark
Of that will be avoided.

  *Regulus.*      If we need,
We have commission to possess the palace,
Enlarge prince Drusus, and make him our chief.

  *Macro.* [*Aside.*] That secret would have burnt his reverend

155    mouth,
Had he not spit it out now. By the gods,
You carry things too—let me borrow'a man
Or two, to bear these—that of freeing Drusus,
Caesar projected as the last and utmost,
Not else to be remembered.

       [*Enter servants.*]

160   *Regulus.*      Here are servants.

  *Macro.* [*Gives letters.*] These to Arruntius, these to Lepidus,
This bear to Cotta, this to Latiaris.
If they demand you'of me, say I have ta'en
Fresh horse and am departed. [*Exeunt servants.*] You, my lord,

165 To your colleague, and be you sure to hold him
With long narration of the new fresh favors

---

154 ENLARGE *set free.*

159 LAST AND UTMOST *last resort.*

Meant to Sejanus, his great patron. I,
With trusted Laco here, are for the guards.
Then to divide. For night hath many eyes,
Whereof, though most do sleep, yet some are spies.    [*Exeunt.*]    170

    [*Sejanus's house. Enter*] *Praecones,* [*Tubicines, Tibicines,*]
    *Flamen, Ministri, Sejanus, Terentius, Satrius,* [*Natta,*] *etc.*
  *Praecones.* "Be all profane far hence. Fly fly far off.
Be absent far. Far hence be all profane."
              *Tubicines, Tibicines sound while the Flamen washeth.*
  *Flamen.* We have been faulty but repent us now,
And bring pure hands, pure vestments, and pure minds.
  [*1*] *Minister.* Pure vessels.
  [*2*] *Minister.*         And pure off'rings.
  [*3*] *Minister.*               Garlands pure.    175
  *Flamen.* Bestow your garlands, and, with reverence, place
The vervin on the altar.
  *Praeco.*        Favor your tongues.
*While they sound again, the Flamen takes of the honey with his
finger and tastes, then ministers to all the rest; so of the milk in an
earthen vessel, he deals about. Which done, he sprinkleth upon the
altar milk; then imposeth the honey, and kindleth his gums, and after
censing about the altar placeth his censer thereon, into which they
put several branches of poppy, and, the music ceasing, proceed.*
  *Flamen.* "Great mother Fortune, queen of human state,
Rectress of action, arbitress of fate,
To whom all sway, all power, all empire bows,    180
Be present, and propitious to our vows."
  *Praeco.* Favor it with your tongues.
  *Minister.* Be present, and propitious to our vows.

177 VERVIN *boughs and leafage used in sacrificing.* FAVOR YOUR TONGUES
    *Jonson's rendering of the ritual phrase* "Favete linguis," *enjoining
    silence so as not to use any word of ill omen.*
179 RECTRESS *governess.*

Act V

Accept our off'ring, and be pleased, great goddess.
  *Terentius.* See, see, the image stirs!
185   *Satrius.*                              And turns away!
  *Natta.* Fortune averts her face!
  *Flamen.*                          Avert, you gods,
The prodigy. Still! Still! Some pious rite
We have neglected. Yet! Heav'n, be appeased.
And be all tokens false, or void, that speak
Thy present wrath.
190   *Sejanus.*          Be thou dumb, scrupulous priest,
And gather up thyself, with these thy wares,
Which I, in spite of thy blind mistress, or
Thy juggling mystery, religion, throw
Thus scornèd on the earth.

                    [*Overturns the statue and the altar.*]
                    Nay, hold thy look
195 Averted, till I woo thee; turn again;
And thou shalt stand to all posterity
Th'eternal game and laughter, with thy neck
Writhed to thy tail, like a ridiculous cat.
Avoid these fumes, these superstitious lights,
200 And all these coz'ning ceremonies, you,
Your pure and spicèd conscience!

      [*Exeunt all but Sejanus, Terentius, Satrius, and Natta.*]
                          I, the slave
And mock of fools? Scorn on my worthy head!
That have been titled and adored a god—
Yea, sacrificed unto myself, in Rome,
205 No less than Jove—and I be brought to do

193 JUGGLING MYSTERY *cheating profession.*
199 AVOID *away with.*
200 COZ'NING *deceitful.*
201 SPICÈD *fastidious.*

A peevish giglot rites? Perhaps the thought
And shame of that made Fortune turn her face,
Knowing herself the lesser deity,
And but my servant. Bashful queen, if so,
Sejanus thanks thy modesty. Who's that?                          210
           *[Enter] Pomponius [and] Minutius.*
  *Pomponius.* His fortune suffers, till he hears my news.
I'have waited here too long. Macro, my lord—
  *Sejanus.* Speak lower, and withdraw.
  *Terentius.*                      Are these things true?
  *Minutius.* Thousands are gazing at it in the streets.
  *Sejanus.* What's that?
  *Terentius.*          Minutius tells us here, my lord,          215
That, a new head being set upon your statue,
A rope is since found wreathed about it. And
But now, a fiery meteor, in the form
Of a great ball, was seen to roll along
The troubled air, where yet it hangs, unperfect,                 220
Th'amazing wonder of the multitude!
  *Sejanus.* No more. That Macro's come, is more than all!
  *Terentius.* Is Macro come?
  *Pomponius.*            I saw him.
  *Terentius.*                   Where? With whom?
  *Pomponius.* With Regulus.
  *Sejanus.*              Terentius—
  *Terentius.*                My lord?
  *Sejanus.* Send for the tribunes. We will straight have up     225
More of the soldiers, for our guard.      *[Exit Terentius.]*
                   Minutius,
We pray you, go for Cotta, Latiaris,
Trio the consul, or what senators

206 GIGLOT *strumpet.*
220 UNPERFECT *arrested in its course.*

Act V

You know are sure, and ours.                    [*Exit Minutius.*]
                    You, my good Natta,
For Laco, provost of the watch.                  [*Exit Natta.*]
230                              Now, Satrius,
The time of proof comes on. Arm all our servants,
And without tumult. [*Exit Satrius.*] You, Pomponius,
Hold some good correspondence with the consul.
Attempt him, noble friend. [*Exit Pomponius.*] These things begin
235  To look like dangers, now, worthy my fates.
Fortune, I see thy worst. Let doubtful states
And things uncertain hang upon thy will.
Me surest death shall render certain still.
Yet, why is now my thought turnèd toward death,
240  Whom fates have let go on so far in breath,
Unchecked or unreproved? I, that did help
To fell the lofty cedar of the world,
Germanicus; that at one stroke cut down
Drusus, that upright elm; withered his vine;
245  Laid Silius and Sabinus, two strong oaks,
Flat on the earth; besides those other shrubs,
Cordus, and Sosia, Claudia Pulchra,
Furnius, and Gallus, which I have grubbed up;
And since, have set my axe so strong and deep
250  Into the root of spreading Agrippine;
Lopped off and scattered her proud branches—Nero,
Drusus, and Caius too, although replanted—
If you will, destinies, that after all,
I faint now ere I touch my period,

231 PROOF *testing.*
238 ME . . . STILL *Death, which is irreversible, will continue to be my instrument
        of safeguard.*
244 VINE *his wife, Livia.*
254 PERIOD *goal.*

You are but cruel; and I already'have done                          255
Things great enough. All Rome hath been my slave.
The Senate sat an idle looker-on
And witness of my power, when I have blushed
More to command, than it to suffer. All
The fathers have sat ready and prepared                             260
To give me empire, temples, or their throats,
When I would ask 'em. And, what crowns the top,
Rome, Senate, people, all the world have seen
Jove but my equal, Caesar but my second.
'Tis then your malice, fates, who, but your own,                    265
Envy and fear t'have any power long known.          [*Exit.*]
        [*Enter*] *Terentius* [*and*] *Tribunes.*
  *Terentius.* Stay here. I'll give his lordship you are come.
        [*Enter*] *Minutius, Cotta,* [*and*] *Latiaris.*
  *Minutius.* Marcus Terentius, pray you tell my lord
Here's Cotta and Latiaris.
  *Terentius.*        Sir, I shall.          [*Exit.*]
     [*Cotta and Latiaris*] *confer their letters.*
  *Cotta.* My letter is the very same with yours,                 270
Only requires me to be present there,
And give my voice to strengthen his design.
  *Latiaris.* Names he not what it is?
  *Cotta.*         No, nor to you.
  *Latiaris.* 'Tis strange and singular doubtful.
  *Cotta.*        So it is.
It may be all is left to lord Sejanus.                              275
        [*Enter*] *Natta* [*and*] *Laco.*
  *Natta.* Gentlemen, where's my lord?
  *Tribunus.*        We wait him here.
  *Cotta.* The provost Laco! What's the news?

267 GIVE *notify.*
274 SINGULAR DOUBTFUL *oddly ambiguous.*

Act V

    *Latiaris.*                            My lord—
                *[Enter] Sejanus.*
    *Sejanus.* Now, my right dear, noble, and trusted friends,
How much I am a captive to your kindness!

280 Most worthy Cotta, Latiaris; Laco,
Your valiant hand; and gentlemen, your loves.
I wish I could divide myself unto you,
Or that it lay within our narrow powers
To satisfy for so enlargèd bounty.

285 Gracinus, we must pray you, hold your guards
Unquit, when morning comes. Saw you the consul?
    *Minutius.* Trio will presently be here, my lord.
    *Cotta.* They are but giving order for the edict,
To warn the Senate.
    *Sejanus.*        How! The Senate?
    *Latiaris.*                    Yes.
This morning, in Apollo's temple.

290    *Cotta.*                We
Are charged by letter to be there, my lord.
    *Sejanus.* By letter? Pray you let's see!
    *Latiaris.*               Knows not his lordship?
    *Cotta.* It seems so!
    *Sejanus.*        A Senate warned? Without my knowledge?
And on this sudden? Senators by letters
Required to be there! Who brought these?

295    *Cotta.*               Macro.
    *Sejanus.* Mine enemy! And when?
    *Cotta.*            This midnight.
    *Sejanus.*                Time,
With ev'ry other circumstance, doth give

286 UNQUIT *undispersed, ready for action.*
293 WARNED *called into session.*
297 GIVE *indicate.*

It hath some strain of engine in't!—How now?

               *[Enter] Satrius.*

  *Satrius.* My lord, Sertorius Macro is without,

Alone, and prays t'have private conference          300

In business of high nature with your lordship,

He says to me, and which regards you much.

  *Sejanus.* Let him come here.

  *Satrius.*               Better, my lord, withdraw.

You will betray what store and strength of friends

Are now about you, which he comes to spy.        305

  *Sejanus.* Is he not armed?

  *Satrius.*           We'll search him.

  *Sejanus.*                     No, but take

And lead him to some room, where you, concealed,

May keep a guard upon us. *[Exit Satrius.]* Noble Laco,

You are our trust, and till our own cohorts

Can be brought up, your strengths must be our guard.   310

                       *He salutes them humbly.*

Now, good Minutius, honored Latiaris,

Most worthy, and my most unwearied friends,

I return instantly.                    *[Exit.]*

  *Latiaris.*     Most worthy lord!

  *Cotta.* His lordship is turned instant kind, methinks.

I'have not observed it in him heretofore.        315

  *[1] Tribunus.* 'Tis true, and it becomes him nobly.

  *Minutius.*                       I

Am rapt withal.

  *[2] Tribunus.* By Mars, he has my lives,

Were they a million, for this only grace.

298 ENGINE *trickery.*
307 SOME ROOM *N.*
318 THIS ONLY GRACE *this graciousness alone.*

Act V

*Laco.* Aye, and to name a man!

*Latiaris.*           As he did me!

*Minutius.* And me!

320    *Latiaris.*      Who would not spend his life and fortunes
To purchase but the look of such a lord?

    *Laco.* [*Aside.*] He that would nor be lord's fool, nor the world's.

         [*Enter*] *Sejanus, Macro,* [*and Satrius.*]

    *Sejanus.* Macro! Most welcome, as most coveted friend!
Let me enjoy my longings. When arrived you?

    *Macro.* About the noon of night.

325    *Sejanus.*            Satrius, give leave.

                  [*Exit Satrius.*]

    *Macro.* I have been, since I came, with both the consuls,
On a particular design from Caesar.

    *Sejanus.* How fares it with our great and royal master?

    *Macro.* Right plentifully well, as with a prince

330 That still holds out the great proportion
Of his large favors, where his judgment hath
Made once divine election. Like the god
That wants not, nor is wearied to bestow
Where merit meets his bounty, as it doth

335 In you, already most happy,'and ere
The sun shall climb the south, most high Sejanus.
Let not my lord be'amused. For to this end
Was I by Caesar sent for, to the isle,
With special caution to conceal my journey;

340 And thence had my dispatch as privately
Again to Rome; charged to come here by night,

319 NAME *call by name.*
322 NOR . . . NOR *neither . . . nor.*
325 NOON OF NIGHT *midnight.*
333 WANTS NOT *lacks nothing.*
337 AMUSED *mystified.*

156

And only to the consuls make narration
Of his great purpose; that the benefit
Might come more full and striking, by how much
It was less looked for or aspired by you,     345
Or least informèd to the common thought.
   *Sejanus.* What may this be? Part of myself, dear Macro!
If good, speak out, and share with your Sejanus.
   *Macro.* If bad, I should for ever loathe myself
To be the messenger to so good a lord.     350
I do exceed m'instructions, to acquaint
Your lordship with thus much, but 'tis my venture
On your retentive wisdom, and because
I would no jealous scruple should molest
Or rack your peace of thought. For I assure     355
My noble lord, no senator yet knows
The business meant; though all, by several letters,
Are warnèd to be there, and give their voices,
Only to add unto the state and grace
Of what is purposed.
   *Sejanus.*      You take pleasure, Macro,     360
Like a coy wench, in torturing your lover.
What can be worth this suffering?
   *Macro.*           That which follows:
The tribunicial dignity and power,
Both which Sejanus is to have this day
Conferred upon him, and by public Senate.     365
   *Sejanus.* Fortune, be mine again. Thou'hast satisfied
For thy suspected loyalty.

346 INFORMÈD . . . THOUGHT *made generally known.*
352–3 'TIS . . . WISDOM *I take the risk of counting on your discretion.*
354 JEALOUS *fearful, anxious.*
357 SEVERAL *separate.*
359 STATE AND GRACE *dignity and favor.*
363 TRIBUNICIAL DIGNITY *N.*

Act V

    *Macro.*               My lord,
I have no longer time. The day approacheth,
And I must back to Caesar.
    *Sejanus.*            Where's Caligula?
370     *Macro.* That I forgot to tell your lordship. Why,
He lingers yonder, about Capreae,
Disgraced. Tiberius hath not seen him yet.
He needs would thrust himself to go with me
Against my wish or will, but I have quitted
375 His forward trouble with as tardy note
As my neglect or silence could afford him.
Your lordship cannot now command me aught,
Because I take no knowledge that I saw you.
But I shall boast to live to serve your lordship,
And so take leave.
380     *Sejanus.*       Honest and worthy Macro,
Your love and friendship. [*Exit Macro.*] Who's there? Satrius,
Attend my honorable friend forth. Oh,
How vain and vile a passion is this fear!
What base, uncomely things it makes men do!
385 Suspect their noblest friends, as I did this,
Flatter poor enemies, entreat their servants,
Stoop, court, and catch at the benevolence
Of creatures unto whom, within this hour,
I would not have vouchsafed a quarter-look,
390 Or piece of face. By you that fools call gods,
Hang all the sky with your prodigious signs,
Fill earth with monsters, drop the scorpion down
Out of the zodiac, or the fiercer lion!

376 afford him] bestow Q

---

374 QUITTED *repaid.*
375 FORWARD *officious.* NOTE *acknowledgment.*
389 QUARTER-LOOK *sidelong glance.*

Shake off the loosened globe from her long hinge,
Roll all the world in darkness, and let loose                    395
Th'enragèd winds to turn up groves and towns!
When I do fear again, let me be struck
With forkèd fire, and unpitied die!
Who fears, is worthy of calamity.                    [*Exit.*]

[*Enter Terentius, Minutius, Laco, Cotta, Latiaris and*] Pomponius,
    *Regulus, Trio, [and others, all from different sides.*]

*Pomponius.* Is not my lord here?
*Terentius.*                    Sir, he will be straight.        400
*Cotta.* What news, Fulcinius Trio?
*Trio.*                    Good, good tidings.
But keep it to yourself. My lord Sejanus
Is to receive this day, in open Senate,
The tribunicial dignity.
*Cotta.*                    Is't true?
*Trio.* No words—not to your thought—but sir, believe it.    405
*Latiaris.* What says the consul?
*Cotta.*                    Speak it not again.
He tells me that today my lord Sejanus—
*Trio.* I must entreat you, Cotta, on your honor
Not to reveal it.
*Cotta.*        On my life, sir.
*Latiaris.*                    Say.
*Cotta.* Is to receive the tribunicial power.                410
But as you are an honorable man,
Let me conjure you not to utter it,
For it is trusted to me with that bond.
*Latiaris.* I am Harpocrates.
*Terentius.*                    Can you assure it?
415    *Pomponius.* The consul told it me, but keep it close.

413 WITH THAT BOND *on that condition.*
414 HARPOCRATES *god of silence and secrecy.*

## Act V

*Minutius.* Lord Latiaris, what's the news?
*Latiaris.*                                        I'll tell you,
But you must swear to keep it secret—
                    [*Enter*] *Sejanus.*
    *Sejanus.* I knew the fates had on their distaff left
More of our thread, than so.
    *Regulus.*                          Hail, great Sejanus!
    *Trio.* Hail, the most honored!
    *Cotta.*                                    Happy!
420    *Latiaris.*                                        High Sejanus!
    *Sejanus.* Do you bring prodigies too?
    *Trio.*                                        May all presage
Turn to those fair effects, whereof we bring
Your lordship news.
    *Regulus.*            May't please my lord withdraw.
    *Sejanus.* Yes. (*To some that stand by.*) I will speak with you anon.
    *Terentius.*                                                My lord,
What is your pleasure for the tribunes?
425    *Sejanus.*                                    Why,
Let 'em be thanked and sent away:
    *Minutius.*                          My lord—
    *Laco.* Will't please your lordship to command me—
    *Sejanus.*                                            No.
You'are troublesome.
    *Minutius.*            The mood is changed.
    [*1*] *Tribunus.*                          Not speak?
    [*2*] *Tribunus.* Nor look?
    *Laco.*                  Aye, he is wise, will make him friends
430 Of such who never love but for their ends.        [*Exeunt.*]
[*Before the Temple of Apollo. Enter*] *Arruntius* [*and*] *Lepidus, divers
                other senators passing by them.*

419 THAN SO *than thus, i.e. than it appeared.*

*Arruntius.* Aye, go, make haste. Take heed you be not last
To tender your "All hail!" in the wide hall
Of huge Sejanus. Run a lictor's pace.
Stay not to put your robes on, but away,
With the pale troubled ensigns of great friendship            435
Stamped i'your face! Now, Marcus Lepidus,
You still believe your former augury?
Sejanus must go downward? You perceive
His wane approaching fast?
   *Lepidus.*           Believe me, Lucius,
I wonder at this rising.
   *Arruntius.*        Aye, and that we               440
Must give our suffrage to it. You will say,
It is to make his fall more steep and grievous—
It may be so. But think it they that can
With idle wishes 'say to bring back time.
In cases desperate, all hope is crime.                       445
See, see! What troops of his officious friends
Flock to salute my lord! And start before
My great proud lord, to get a lordlike nod!
Attend my lord unto the Senate House!
Bring back my lord! Like servile ushers, make               450
Way for my lord! Proclaim his idol lordship
More than ten criers or six noise of trumpets!
Make legs, kiss hands, and take a scattered hair
From my lord's eminent shoulder! See Sanquinius,
With his slow belly, and his dropsy, look                    455
What toiling haste he makes! Yet here's another,

454 eminent] excellent Q

443 THINK IT *let them think it.*
444 'SAY *essay.*
452 NOISE *bands.*
453 MAKE LEGS *bow.*

Act V

Retarded with the gout, will be afore him!
Get thee Liburnian porters, thou gross fool,
To bear thy'obsequious fatness, like thy peers.
460 They'are met! The gout returns, and his great carriage.

          *Lictors, consuls, Sejanus, etc. pass over the stage.*

    *Lictores.* Give way! Make place! Room for the consul!
    *Sanquinius.*                                       Hail,
Hail, great Sejanus!
    *Haterius.*            Hail, my honored lord!
    *Arruntius.* We shall be marked anon, for our not-hail.
    *Lepidus.* That is already done.
    *Arruntius.*                 It is a note
465 Of upstart greatness to observe and watch
For these poor trifles, which the noble mind
Neglects and scorns.
    *Lepidus.*            Aye, and they think themselves
Deeply dishonored, where they are omitted,
As if they were necessities that helped
470 To the perfection of their dignities,
And hate the men that but refrain 'em.
    *Arruntius.*             Oh,
There is a farther cause of hate. Their breasts
Are guilty that we know their obscure springs
And base beginnings. Thence the anger grows.
On. Follow.                             *[Exeunt.]*

           *[Enter] Macro [and] Laco.*

475     *Macro.* When all are entered, shut the temple doors,
And bring your guards up to the gate.

---

458 LIBURNIAN PORTERS "*Illyrian slaves who acted as court-messengers. A
    particular kind of sedan-chair, the liburna, was named after them*"
    (*Herford and Simpson 9,630*).
464 NOTE *sign.*
473 SPRINGS *origins.*

*Laco.*                              I will.

*Macro.* If you shall hear commotion in the Senate,
Present yourself, and charge on any man
Shall offer to come forth.

*Laco.*                    I am instructed.                    [*Exeunt.*]

*The Senate.*

[*In the Temple of Apollo. Enter*] *Haterius, Trio, Sanquinius, Cotta,
Regulus, Sejanus, Pomponius, Latiaris, Lepidus, Arruntius,
Praecones, Lictores,* [*and other senators*].

*Haterius.* How well his lordship looks today!

*Trio.*                              As if                          480
He had been born, or made for this hour's state.

*Cotta.* Your fellow consul's come about, methinks?

*Trio.* Aye, he is wise.

*Sanquinius.*            Sejanus trusts him well.

*Trio.* Sejanus is a noble, bounteous lord.

*Haterius.* He is so, and most valiant.

*Latiaris.*                       And most wise.                    485

[*1*] *Senator.* He's everything.

*Latiaris.*                    Worthy of all, and more
Than bounty can bestow.

*Trio.*                 This dignity
Will make him worthy.

*Pomponius.*          Above Caesar.

*Sanquinius.*                      Tut,
Caesar is but the rector of an isle,
He of the empire.

*Trio.*           Now he will have power                            490
More to reward than ever.

*Cotta.*                   Let us look

481 STATE *dignity.*
489 RECTOR *ruler.*

Act V

We be not slack in giving him our voices.

   *Latiaris.* Not I.

   *Sanquinius.*   Nor I.

   *Cotta.*         The readier we seem
To propagate his honors, will more bind
His thought to ours.

495   *Haterius.*      I think right with your lordship.
It is the way to have us hold our places.

   *Sanquinius.* Aye, and get more.

   *Latiaris.*         More office, and more titles.

   *Pomponius.* I will not lose the part I hope to share
In these his fortunes, for my patrimony.

500   *Latiaris.* See how Arruntius sits, and Lepidus.

   *Trio.* Let 'em alone, they will be marked anon.

   [1] *Senator.* I'll do with others.

   [2] *Senator.*     So will I.

   [3] *Senator.*     And I.

Men grow not in the state, but as they are planted
Warm in his favors.

   *Cotta.*    Noble Sejanus!

   *Haterius.* Honored Sejanus!

505   *Latiaris.*     Worthy and great Sejanus!

   *Arruntius.* Gods! How the sponges open, and take in,
And shut again! Look, look! Is not he blest
That gets a seat in eye-reach of him? More,
That comes in ear-, or tongue-reach? Oh, but most
510 Can claw his subtle elbow, or with a buzz
Flyblow his ears.

   [1] *Praeco.*   Proclaim the Senate's peace,
And give last summons by the edict.

511 *Praeco.*] PRAET. Q,F

493–5 THE . . . OURS *The more we show ourselves eager to multiply his honors,
the more we will endear ourselves to him.*

[2] *Praeco.*                                         Silence!

In the name of Caesar and the Senate, silence!

"Memmius Regulus, and Fulcinius Trio, consuls, these present
kalends of June, with the first light, shall hold a Senate in the    [515]
Temple of Apollo Palatine. All that are fathers, and are registered
fathers, that have right of entering the Senate, we warn or command you be frequently present. Take knowledge the business
is the commonwealth's. Whosoever is absent, his fine or mulct    [520]
will be taken; his excuse will not be taken."

    *Trio.* Note who are absent, and record their names.

    *Regulus.* Fathers conscript, may what I am to utter
Turn good and happy for the commonwealth.
And thou Apollo, in whose holy house                              525
We here are met, inspire us all with truth,
And liberty of censure, to our thought.
The majesty of great Tiberius Caesar
Propounds to this grave Senate the bestowing
Upon the man he loves, honored Sejanus,                          530
The tribunicial dignity and power.
Here are his letters, signèd with his signet.
What pleaseth now the fathers to be done?

    *Senators.* Read, read 'em; open; publicly read 'em.

    *Cotta.* Caesar hath honored his own greatness much       535
In thinking of this act.

    *Trio.*                    It was a thought
Happy, and worthy Caesar.

    *Latiaris.*                    And the lord
As worthy it, on whom it is directed!

    *Haterius.* Most worthy!

---

530 loves] lones Q

---

515 KALENDS *first day of the month.*
516–7 REGISTERED FATHERS *conscript fathers.*
518 FREQUENTLY *in full force.*

Act V

   *Sanquinius.*           Rome did never boast the virtue
540 That could give envy bounds, but his: Sejanus—
   [*1*] *Senator.* Honored, and noble!
   [*2*] *Senator.*         Good and great Sejanus!
   *Arruntius.* [*Aside.*] Oh, most tame slavery and fierce flattery!
   *Praeco.*                      Silence!

*The epistle is read.*

### "TIBERIUS CAESAR
To the Senate:
545              Greeting.

If you, conscript fathers, with your children, be in health, it is
abundantly well. We with our friends here are so. The care of
the commonwealth, howsoever we are removed in person,
cannot be absent to our thought, although oftentimes, even to
[550] princes most present, the truth of their own affairs is hid; than
which nothing falls out more miserable to a state, or makes the
art of governing more difficult. But since it hath been our easeful
happiness to enjoy both the aids and industry of so vigilant a
Senate, we profess to have been the more indulgent to our
[555] pleasures, not as being careless of our office, but rather secure of
the necessity. Neither do these common rumors of many and
infamous libels published against our retirement at all afflict us,
being born more out of men's ignorance than their malice; and
will, neglected, find their own grave quickly; whereas too
[560] sensibly acknowledged, it would make their obloquy ours. Nor
do we desire their authors, though found, be censured, since in
a free state (as ours) all men ought to enjoy their minds and
tongues free."

   *Arruntius.* [*Aside.*] The lapwing, the lapwing!

560 SENSIBLY ACKNOWLEDGED *sensitively received.*
564 LAPWING *popularly believed to drag its wing, as if wounded, and call out at
a distance from its nest, so as to divert attention from its young. Arruntius
regards Tiberius' talk of freedom as such a feint.*

166

"Yet in things which shall worthily and more near concern the [565]
majesty of a prince, we shall fear to be so unnaturally cruel to our
fame, as to neglect them. True it is, conscript fathers, that we have
raised Sejanus from obscure and almost unknown gentry—,"

Senators. How? How?

"to the highest and most conspicuous point of greatness, and, we [570]
hope, deservingly. Yet not without danger, it being a most bold
hazard in that sovereign who, by his particular love to one, dares
adventure the hatred of all his other subjects."

Arruntius. [Aside.] This touches; the blood turns.

"But we affy in your loves and understandings, and do no way [575]
suspect the merit of our Sejanus to make our favors offensive to
any."

Senators. Oh! Good, good!

"Though we could have wished his zeal had run a calmer course
against Agrippina and our nephews, howsoever the openness of [580]
their actions declared them delinquents; and that he would have
remembered no innocence is so safe, but it rejoiceth to stand in the
sight of mercy; the use of which in us he hath so quite taken away
toward them by his loyal fury, as now our clemency would be
thought but wearied cruelty, if we should offer to exercise it." [585]

Arruntius. [Aside.] I thank him, there I looked for't. A good fox!

"Some there be that would interpret this his public severity
to be particular ambition; and that under a pretext of service
to us, he doth but remove his own lets; alleging the strengths he [590]
hath made to himself by the praetorian soldiers, by his faction in
court and Senate, by the offices he holds himself and confers on
others, his popularity and dependents, his urging, and almost

575 AFFY trust.
589 PARTICULAR private.
590 LETS hindrances.

driving us to this our unwilling retirement, and lastly his
[595] aspiring to be our son-in-law."

    *Senators.* This's strange!
    *Arruntius.* [*Aside.*] I shall anon believe your vultures, Marcus.

"Your wisdoms, conscript fathers, are able to examine and
censure these suggestions. But were they left to our absolving
[600] voice, we durst pronounce them, as we think them, most
malicious."

    *Senators.* Oh, he has restored all, list.

"Yet are they offered to be averred, and on the lives of the
informers. What we should say, or rather what we should not
[605] say, lords of the Senate, if this be true, our gods and goddesses
confound us if we know! Only we must think we have placed
our benefits ill, and conclude that in our choice either we were
wanting to the gods, or the gods to us."

*The senators shift their places.*

    *Arruntius.* [*Aside.*] The place grows hot, they shift.

[610] "We have not been covetous, honorable fathers, to change.
Neither is it now any new lust that alters our affection, or old
loathing, but those needful jealousies of state, that warn wiser
princes hourly to provide their safety, and do teach them how
learned a thing it is to beware of the humblest enemy—much
[615] more of those great ones whom their own employed favors
have made fit for their fears."

    [1] *Senator.* Away!
    [2] *Senator.*          Sit farther.

599 CENSURE *judge.*
604–6 WHAT . . . KNOW *N.*
612 JEALOUSIES *anxieties.*
613 PROVIDE *provide for.*
614 LEARNED *wise.*

*Cotta.*                              Let's remove—

*Arruntius.* [*Aside.*] Gods! How the leaves drop off, this little wind!

"We therefore desire that the offices he holds be first seized by
the Senate, and himself suspended from all exercise of place or    [620]
power—"

*Senators.* How!

*Sanquinius.* [*Thrusting by.*] By your leave.

*Arruntius.*                              Come, porpoise.

          [*Aside.*] Where's Haterius?

His gout keeps him most miserably constant.

Your dancing shows a tempest.

*Sejanus.*                    Read no more.

*Regulus.* Lords of the Senate, hold your seats. Read on.          625

*Sejanus.* These letters, they are forged.

*Regulus.*                         A guard, sit still.

          *Laco enters with the guards.*

*Arruntius.* There's change.

*Regulus.*              Bid silence, and read forward.

*Praeco.* Silence—"and himself suspended from all exercise of
place or power, but till due and mature trial be made of his
innocency, which yet we can faintly apprehend the necessity        [630]
to doubt. If, conscript fathers, to your more searching wisdoms
there shall appear farther cause—or of farther proceeding,
either to seizure of lands, goods, or more—it is not our power that
shall limit your authority, or our favor that must corrupt your
justice. Either were dishonorable in you, and both uncharitable    [635]
to ourself. We would willingly be present with your counsels in
this business, but the danger of so potent a faction, if it should
prove so, forbids our attempting it, except one of the consuls

627 There's] Here's Q
638 attempting it] attempt Q

---

622 PORPOISE *applied to Sanquinius, fat and awkward, and because the appearance of porpoises was popularly believed to bode stormy weather.*

would be entreated for our safety to undertake the guard of us
[640] home; then we should most readily adventure. In the meantime,
it shall not be fit for us to importune so judicious a Senate, who
know how much they hurt the innocent that spare the guilty, and
how grateful a sacrifice to the gods is the life of an ingrateful
person. We reflect not in this on Sejanus—notwithstanding, if
[645] you keep an eye upon him—and there is Latiaris, a senator, and
Pinnarius Natta, two of his most trusted ministers, and so professed, whom we desire not to have apprênded, but as the
necessity of the cause exacts it."

    *Regulus.* A guard on Latiaris.

650    *Arruntius.*                      Oh, the spy,
The reverend spy is caught! Who pities him?
Reward, sir, for your service. Now you ha' done
Your property, you see what use is made!

                            *[Exeunt Latiaris and Natta, guarded.]*
Hang up the instrument.

    *Sejanus.*              Give leave.

    *Laco.*                    Stand, stand.

655  He comes upon his death that doth advance
An inch toward my point.

    *Sejanus.*          Have we no friends here?

    *Arruntius.*                      Hushed.
Where now are all the hails and acclamations?

                    *[Enter] Macro.*

    *Macro.* Hail to the consuls, and this noble Senate!

    *Sejanus. [Aside.]* Is Macro here? Oh, thou art lost, Sejanus.

---

656 friends] friend Q *originally*

---

640 ADVENTURE *take the risk.*
651 REVEREND *worthy.*
653 PROPERTY *office, function.*
658 HAIL . . . SENATE *Macro's greeting comes as an irony, as though in answer to
    Arruntius' question in the previous line.*

*Macro.* Sit still, and unaffrighted, reverend fathers. 660
Macro, by Caesar's grace the new-made provost,
And now possessed of the praetorian bands,
An honor late belonged to that proud man,
Bids you be safe; and to your constant doom
Of his deservings, offers you the surety 665
Of all the soldiers, tribunes, and centurions
Received in our command.
　　*Regulus.* 　　　　　　Sejanus, Sejanus!
Stand forth, Sejanus!
　　*Sejanus.* 　　　　Am I called?
　　*Macro.* 　　　　　　　　Aye, thou,
Thou insolent monster, art bid stand.
　　*Sejanus.* 　　　　　　　　Why, Macro,
It hath been otherwise between you and I. 670
This court, that knows us both, hath seen a difference,
And can, if it be pleased to speak, confirm
Whose insolence is most.
　　*Macro.* 　　　　　Come down, Typhoeus.
If mine be most, lo, thus I make it more,
Kick up thy heels in air, tear off thy robe, 675
Play with thy beard and nostrils. Thus 'tis fit—
And no man take compassion of thy state—
To use th'ingrateful viper, tread his brains
Into the earth.
　　*Regulus.* 　Forbear.
　　*Macro.* 　　　　　　If I could lose
All my humanity now, 'twere well to torture 680
So meriting a traitor. Wherefore, fathers,

664-5 TO YOUR . . . DESERVINGS *in return for your resolute judgment on his
　　deserts.*
673 TYPHOEUS *Titan who warred against the gods, and was felled by a thunder-
　　bolt from Zeus.*

171

Act V

Sit you amazed and silent, and not censure
This wretch, who in the hour he first rebelled
'Gainst Caesar's bounty, did condemn himself?
685  Phlegra, the field where all the sons of earth
Mustered against the gods, did ne'er acknowledge
So proud and huge a monster.
    *Regulus.*               Take him hence.
And all the gods guard Caesar.
    *Trio.*                  Take him hence.
    *Haterius.* Hence!
    *Cotta.*        To the dungeon with him!
    *Sanquinius.*              He deserves it.
    *Senators.* Crown all our doors with bays.
690      *Sanquinius.*             And let an ox
With gilded horns and garlands, straight be led
Unto the Capitol.
    *Haterius.*      And sacrificed
To Jove for Caesar's safety.
    *Trio.*            All our gods
Be present still to Caesar!
    *Cotta.*         Phoebus!
    *Sanquinius.*         Mars!
    *Haterius.* Diana!
    *Sanquinius.*   Pallas!
695      *Senators.*        Juno, Mercury—
All guard him.
    *Macro.*   Forth, thou prodigy of men!

                             *[Exit Sejanus, guarded.]*

685 PHLEGRA *the scene of the Titans' revolt.*
686 ACKNOWLEDGE *own.*
690 BAYS *as a sign of rejoicing.*
696 FORTH *away.*
696–832 *N.*

172

*Cotta.* Let all the traitor's titles be defaced.
*Trio.* His images and statues be pulled down.
*Haterius.* His chariot wheels be broken.
*Arruntius.*                              And the legs
Of the poor horses, that deservèd naught,                               700
Let them be broken too.
     *Lepidus.*                    Oh, violent change
And whirl of men's affections!
     *Arruntius.*                    Like as both
Their bulks and souls were bound on Fortune's wheel,
And must act only with her motion.
          [*Exeunt all but*] *Lepidus, Arruntius* [*and a few senators.*]
     *Lepidus.* Who would depend upon the popular air,                 705
Or voice of men, that have today beheld
That which if all the gods had foredeclared,
Would not have been believed, Sejanus' fall?
He that this morn rose proudly as the sun,
And breaking through a mist of clients' breath,                        710
Came on as gazed at and admired as he
When superstitious Moors salute his light!
That had our servile nobles waiting him
As common grooms, and hanging on his look,
No less than human life on destiny!                                    715
That had men's knees as frequent as the gods,
And sacrifices more than Rome had altars.
And this man fall! Fall? Aye, without a look
That durst appear his friend, or lend so much
Of vain relief to his changed state, as pity!                          720
     *Arruntius.* They that before, like gnats, played in his beams.

---

704 MUST . . . MOTION *i.e. were incapable of independent action.*
705 POPULAR AIR *favor of the populace.*
713 WAITING *attending on.*

And thronged to circumscribe him, now not seen,
Nor deign to hold a common seat with him.
Others, that waited him unto the Senate,
725 Now inhumanely ravish him to prison,
Whom, but this morn, they followed as their lord!
Guard through the streets, bound like a fugitive;
Instead of wreaths, give fetters; strokes for stoops;
Blind shame for honors; and black taunts for titles.
Who would trust slippery chance?
730    *Lepidus.*                 They that would make
Themselves her spoil, and foolishly forget,
When she doth flatter, that she comes to prey.
Fortune, thou hadst no deity if men
Had wisdom. We have placèd thee so high
735 By fond belief in thy felicity.        *Shout within.*
   *Senators.* The gods guard Caesar! All the gods guard Caesar!
      *[Re-enter] Macro, Regulus, [and] senators.*
   *Macro.* Now, great Sejanus, you that awed the state,
And sought to bring the nobles to your whip,
That would be Caesar's tutor, and dispose
740 Of dignities and offices; that had
The public head still bare to your designs,
And made the general voice to echo yours;
That looked for salutations twelve score off,
And would have pyramids, yea, temples reared
745 To your huge greatness! Now you lie as flat

722 CIRCUMSCRIBE *surround.*
723 COMMON *in common.*
724 WAITED *ceremoniously attended.*
727 FUGITIVE *runaway slave.*
731 SPOIL *booty.*
740–1 THAT HAD . . . DESIGNS *to whom the people always listened with heads respectfully bared.*
743 TWELVE SCORE OFF *twelve score yards away.*

174

As was your pride advanced.
   *Regulus.*                Thanks to the gods.
   *Senators.* And praise to Macro that hath savèd Rome!
Liberty, liberty, liberty! Lead on!
And praise to Macro, that hath savèd Rome!
               *[Exeunt all but] Arruntius and Lepidus.*
   *Arruntius.* I prophesy out of this Senate's flattery       750
That this new fellow, Macro, will become
A greater prodigy in Rome than he
That now is fall'n.
           *[Enter Terentius.]*
   *Terentius.*   O you whose minds are good,
And have not forced all mankind from your breasts,
That yet have so much stock of virtue left         755
To pity guilty states, when they are wretched;
Lend your soft ears to hear, and eyes to weep
Deeds done by men, beyond the acts of furies.
The eager multitude, who never yet
Knew why to love, or hate, but only pleased      760
T'express their rage of power, no sooner heard
The murmur of Sejanus in decline,
But with that speed and heat of appetite
With which they greedily devour the way
To some great sports, or a new theater,        765
They filled the Capitol, and Pompey's Cirque.
Where, like so many mastiffs, biting stones,
As if his statues now were sensive grown
Of their wild fury, first they tear them down,

768 sensive grown] sensitive Q

---

754 MANKIND *humanity.*
759 EAGER *fierce, impetuous.*
766 CIRQUE *circus, stadium.*
768 SENSIVE *able to feel.*

770 Then fastening ropes, drag them along the streets,
Crying in scorn, "This, this was that rich head
Was crowned with garlands and with odors! This
That was in Rome so reverencèd!" Now
The furnace and the bellows shall to work,
775 The great Sejanus crack, and piece by piece,
Drop i'the founder's pit.

    *Lepidus.*          Oh, popular rage!

    *Terentius.* The whilst, the Senate at the temple of Concord
Make haste to meet again, and thronging cry,
"Let us condemn him! Tread him down in water,
780 While he doth lie upon the bank. Away!"
Where some more tardy cry unto their bearers,
"He will be censured ere we come. Run, knaves!"
And use that furious diligence, for fear
Their bondmen should inform against their slackness,
785 And bring their quaking flesh unto the hook.
The rout, they follow with confusèd voice,
Crying, they're glad, say they could ne'er abide him;
Inquire what man he was, what kind of face?
What beard he had? What nose? What lips? Protest
790 They ever did presage h'would come to this;
They never thought him wise nor valiant; ask
After his garments, when he dies; what death.
And not a beast of all the herd demands
What was his crime, or who were his accusers;
795 Under what proof or testimony he fell.
There came—says one—a huge, long, worded letter
From Capreae against him. Did there so?
Oh, they are satisfied; no more.

    *Lepidus.*          Alas!

They follow fortune, and hate men condemned,

795 proof] roof F *originally*

Guilty or not.

    *Arruntius.*   But had Sejanus thrived         800
In his design, and prosperously oppressed
The old Tiberius, then, in that same minute,
These very rascals that now rage like furies
Would have proclaimed Sejanus emperor.

    *Lepidus.* But what hath followed?

    *Terentius.*                   Sentence, by the Senate,   805
To lose his head; which was no sooner off,
But that and th'unfortunate trunk were seized
By the rude multitude; who not content
With what the forward justice of the state
Officiously had done, with violent rage         810
Have rent it limb from limb. A thousand heads,
A thousand hands, ten thousand tongues and voices,
Employed at once in several acts of malice!
Old men not staid with age, virgins with shame,
Late wives with loss of husbands, mothers of children,   815
Losing all grief in joy of his sad fall,
Run quite transported with their cruelty—
These mounting at his head, these at his face,
These digging out his eyes, those with his brain
Sprinkling themselves, their houses, and their friends.   820
Others are met, have ravished thence an arm,
And deal small pieces of the flesh for favors.
These with a thigh; this hath cut off his hands;
And this his feet; these fingers, and these toes.
That hath his liver; he his heart; there wants    825
Nothing but room for wrath, and place for hatred.

809 FORWARD *overzealous.*
810 OFFICIOUSLY *officially.*
813 SEVERAL *separate.*
818 MOUNTING *N.*

Act V

What cannot oft be done, is now o'erdone.
The whole, and all of what was great Sejanus,
And next to Caesar did possess the world,
830   Now torn and scattered, as he needs no grave.
Each little dust covers a little part.
So lies he nowhere, and yet often buried.

                    [*Enter*] *Nuntius.*

   *Arruntius.* More of Sejanus?
   *Nuntius.*                Yes.
   *Lepidus.*                        What can be added?
We know him dead.
   *Nuntius.*              Then there begin your pity.
835   There is enough behind to melt ev'n Rome
And Caesar into tears, since never slave
Could yet so highly'offend, but tyranny,
In torturing him, would make him worth lamenting.
A son and daughter to the dead Sejanus
840   —Of whom there is not now so much remaining
As would give fast'ning to the hangman's hook—
Have they drawn forth for farther sacrifice;
Whose tenderness of knowledge, unripe years,
And childish silly innocence was such,
845   As scarce would lend them feeling of their danger;
The girl so simple, as she often asked
Where they would lead her? For what cause they dragged her?
Cried, she would do no more. That she could take
Warning with beating. And because our laws
850   Admit no virgin immature to die,

---

836 since] though Q

834 THERE . . . PITY N.
839–54 N.
844 SILLY *simple.*

178

The wittily and strangely cruel Macro
Delivered her to be deflow'red and spoiled
By the rude lust of the licentious hangman,
Then to be strangled with her harmless brother.

   *Lepidus.* Oh, act most worthy hell and lasting night,      855
To hide it from the world!

   *Nuntius.*               Their bodies thrown
Into the Gemonies—I know not how,
Or by what accident returned—the mother,
Th'expulsèd Apicata, finds them there;
Whom when she saw lie spread on the degrees,      860
After a world of fury on herself,
Tearing her hair, defacing of her face,
Beating her breasts and womb, kneeling amazed,
Crying to heaven, then to them; at last,
Her drownèd voice gat up above her woes,      865
And with such black and bitter execrations
As might affright the gods, and force the sun
Run backward to the east—nay, make the old
Deformèd Chaos rise again, t'o'erwhelm
Them, us, and all the world—she fills the air;      870
Upbraids the heavens with their partial dooms;
Defies their tyrannous powers; and demands
What she and those poor innocents have transgressed,
That they must suffer such a share in vengeance,
Whilst Livia, Lygdus, and Eudemus live—      875
Who, as she says, and firmly vows to prove it
To Caesar and the Senate, poisoned Drusus.

851 WITTILY *ingeniously.* STRANGELY *abnormally.*
858–77 N.
859 EXPULSÈD *divorced.*
860 DEGREES *stairs.*
863 AMAZED *crazed.*
871 PARTIAL DOOMS *unjust decrees.*

Act V

    *Lepidus.* Confederates with her husband?
    *Nuntius.*                            Aye.
    *Lepidus.*                          Strange act!
    *Arruntius.* And strangely opened. What says now my monster,
880 The multitude? They reel now, do they not?
    *Nuntius.* Their gall is gone, and now they 'gin to weep
The mischief they have done.
    *Arruntius.*             I thank 'em, rogues!
    *Nuntius.* Part are so stupid, or so flexible,
As they believe him innocent. All grieve.
885 And some, whose hands yet reek with his warm blood,
And gripe the part which they did tear of him,
Wish him collected and created new.
    *Lepidus.* How Fortune plies her sports, when she begins
To practice 'em! Pursues, continues, adds!
890 Confounds, with varying her impassioned moods!
    *Arruntius.* Dost thou hope, Fortune, to redeem thy crimes?
To make amends for thy ill-placèd favors,
With these strange punishments? Forbear, you things,
That stand upon the pinnacles of state,
895 To boast your slippery height. When you do fall,
You pash yourselves in pieces, ne'er to rise,
And he that lends you pity is not wise.
    *Terentius.* Let this example move th'insolent man
Not to grow proud and careless of the gods.
900 It is an odious wisdom to blaspheme,
Much more to slighten or deny their powers.
For whom the morning saw so great and high,
Thus low and little, 'fore the'even doth lie.       [*Exeunt.*]

879 OPENED *revealed.*
881 GALL *malice.*
893 STRANGE *exceptional.*
896 PASH *smash.*

THE END

# Notes

The notes that follow will include substantial extracts from Tacitus'
*Annals of Imperial Rome*, in the translation by Michael Grant, Penguin
Classics L 60 (rev. ed. London, 1959, reprinted by kind permission of the
publishers, Penguin Books Ltd.) and a few comments on these extracts.
The purpose of the excerpts and comment is to give a partial idea of how
Jonson dealt with his main source; how, when he transferred detail from
Tacitus into his play, he utilized what he borrowed. With respect to this
topic, the reader should observe certain cautions. First, Tacitus is only one,
although the chief, among a multitude of sources. Jonson consulted other
historians—Suetonius, Dio Cassius, Velleius Paterculus, Plutarch—and
paraphrased from nonhistorical writings as well, the plays of Seneca, the
satires of Juvenal and Persius, the poems of Virgil and Claudian, and much
else, giving rise to Hazlitt's well-known description of the play as "an
admirable piece of ancient mosaic." Undoubtedly Jonson wished his more
knowing readers to enjoy discovering familiar passages from the ancients
wrought into a complex new fabric, somewhat as Milton expected readers
to appreciate in *Lycidas* its sophisticated allusiveness to centuries of pastoral
elegy. The bulk and variety of Jonson's sources make full annotation of
them impossible here; for a complete accounting the reader is referred to
the editions of Briggs and of Herford and Simpson.

Second, the Tacitus material itself is not presented complete. Numerous
scattered phrases, sentences, and paragraphs remain unreproduced. At a
guess, the present notes include about 90 per cent of those portions that can
legitimately be regarded as "source." Readers should bear in mind,
further, that what Jonson chooses to ignore is often as interesting as an
index to his intentions as what he includes, and that a passage assembled
from scattered hints may outrank in interest one traceable to a single

identifiable passage. Finally, it should be noted that Jonson used Tacitus in the 1600 edition of Justus Lipsius, in which the method of presentation—the footnotes, marginal summaries, and "breviaries" or epitomes of chapters printed as headnotes—often directed his attention to one aspect or another of his material, or even suggested interpretations of it. For an exact accounting of Jonson's use of his source, one would want to scrutinize it in Lipsius' edition, in the form in which Jonson himself had access to it. On this see Ellen M. T. Duffy, "Ben Jonson's Debt to Renaissance Scholarship in *Sejanus* and *Catiline*," *Modern Language Review*, 42 (1947), 26–29, and, more importantly, Daniel Boughner, "Jonson's Use of Lipsius in *Sejanus*," *Modern Language Notes*, 73 (1958), 247–55. The woodcut reproduced as frontispiece is from the Life of Tiberius in a sixteenth-century edition of Suetonius' *Lives of the Caesars*, with commentary by Filippo Beroaldo (Venice, 1510). It illustrates Tiberius' cruelty toward Sejanus' friends after Sejanus' fall, and is reproduced with the kind permission of the General Library of the University of California at Berkeley.

#### DEDICATION

ESME, LORD AUBIGNY *One of Jonson's noble patrons, with whom he was living at the time of the composition of* Sejanus, *apparently to some extent in refuge from his wife (see* Conversations with Drummond of Hawthornden, *lines 254–55). Epigram CXXVII contains a grateful acknowledgment of Aubigny's hospitality.*

#### TO THE READERS

5–6 NO TRUE . . . TIME *Does not adhere to the "unity of time"—does not confine its action to the space of a single day—and hence is not a "true" or authentic tragedy.*

9 LAWS *Jonson refers here not only to the unities of place and time but to all the rules for tragedy formulated by sixteenth-century critics, especially the Italian commentators upon Aristotle. In defending himself for having omitted a chorus, Jonson points out that none of those who have in his own day tried to introduce the chorus have had much success with it.*

9–13 NOR IS . . . DELIGHT *"It is neither necessary nor possible nowadays, given the nature of the audiences of the public theater, to recreate tragedy in its ancient dignity and ceremony and still please the people." Jonson's remark embodies the dilemma he felt himself to be in, wishing to write a "true" tragedy following the best critics, but wishing to write it for the public stage.*

16 TRUTH OF ARGUMENT *Strict adherence to historical fact. This was Jonson's more stringent interpretation of the general precept, laid down by Renaissance critics, that tragedy should utilize plots drawn from history.*

41 A SECOND PEN *Sometimes thought to have been that of George Chapman, for whom Jonson had considerable respect, and whose own historical tragedies resemble Jonson's more closely than any others of the period. But no real clue exists as to the identity of the collaborator, or as to which portions of the original play were his work.*

THE ARGUMENT

17 *The following symbols will be used in the textual notes: Q designates a Quarto variant. F designates a Folio reading that has been corrected by a reading from the Quarto. Q,F designates a reading common to both Quarto and Folio that has been emended on the precedent of a later edition. Variants and rejected readings recorded in the textual notes will be modernized.*

37 THE PEOPLE *Q adds here a final paragraph, omitted in F: "This do we advance as a mark of terror to all traitors and treasons, to show how just the heavens are in pouring and thundering down a weighty vengeance on their unnatural intents, even to the worst princes, much more to those for guard of whose piety and virtue the angels are in continual watch, and God himself miraculously working." Sejanus had evidently been thought subversive, to judge from the fact that it apparently caused Jonson to be summoned before the Privy Council on charges of treason. Probably the Quarto text expunged the main offending passages—which may, of course, have been the work of Jonson's collaborator as well as of Jonson—but enough remains, even in the printed version, of Jonson's sharp comment on despotic rulers to account for the anger of a thin-skinned government (see Herford and Simpson, 9, 587–91, for a collection of relevant passages). Between the first performance of the play, in 1603, and its publication in 1605, probably occurred the Gunpowder Plot, and Jonson most likely found it expedient to include such tangible evidence of his loyalty as this sentence. When he came later to revise for the Folio, the dangerous moment had passed and he could omit the passage.*

THE PERSONS OF THE PLAY

*For a succinct account of each of these, based on the information in Tacitus, see Herford and Simpson, 9, 594–97. See also above, Introduction.*

Act I

36 HIS WATCH . . . CLOCK *The Romans had waterclocks and sundials, and
sometimes signaled the hour by means of trumpet calls or slaves announcing
the time, but the reference to watches would seem to be an anachronism.*

41–55 *Tacitus, Annals 3.65: "But this was a tainted, meanly obsequious age.
The greatest figures had to protect their positions by subserviency; and, in
addition to them, all ex-consuls, most ex-praetors, even many junior senators
competed with each other's offensively sycophantic proposals. There is a
tradition that whenever Tiberius left the senate-house he exclaimed in Greek,
' Men fit to be slaves!' Even he, freedom's enemy, became impatient of such
abject servility" (Grant, p. 147). The adaptation utilizes a common device
of Jonson's: it transfers sentiments from Tacitus himself to one or another of
the characters in the play. Although a close paraphrase, it also illustrates
Jonson's tendency to make the rhythm taut, the tone stinging, and the
rhetorical arrangement climactic—here leading from the corrupted gentry
through the "Senators that else use not their voices" to the culminating
detail, the rejection of them all by Tiberius.*

48 SENATORS . . . VOICES *"Pedarii," glosses Jonson marginally, referring to
those senators who had not yet been officially enrolled, hence had as yet no
authority to speak, yet would infringe the rules in order to flatter Tiberius
along with the rest.*

56–74, 85–104 *Neither of these passages has a specific source. They represent
Jonson's attempt to explain the decline in Roman freedom by ascribing it to a
deterioration of moral fiber on the part of the Romans themselves.*

91 WHEN . . . EVIL *One of several comments in Jonson that indicate his un-
favorable view of Julius Caesar. See the character of Caesar in* Catiline.

128–54 *Tacitus, Annals 2.72–73: "The province and surrounding peoples
grieved greatly. Foreign countries and kings mourned his friendliness to allies
and forgiveness to enemies. Both his looks and his words had inspired respect.
Yet his dignity and grandeur, befitting his lofty rank, had been unaccompanied
by any arrogance or jealousy. At his funeral there was no procession of
statues. But there were abundant eulogies and reminiscences of his fine
character. Some felt that his appearance, short life, and manner of death (like
its locality) recalled Alexander the Great. Both were handsome, both died
soon after thirty, both succumbed to the treachery of compatriots in a foreign
land. But Germanicus, it was added, was kind to his friends, modest in his
pleasures, a man with one wife and legitimate children. Though not so rash*

*as Alexander, he was no less of a warrior. Only, after defeating the Germans many times, he had not been allowed to complete their subjection. If he had been in sole control, with royal power and title, he would have equalled Alexander in military renown as easily as he outdid him in clemency, self-control, and every other good quality"* (Grant, p. 111).

132 IMAGES AND POMP *At Roman funerals it was customary for relatives of the deceased to wear masks, or "images," of him and his ancestors. The family masks being at Rome, and Drusus dying at Antioch, the custom could not in the present case have been observed.*

139 PARALLELED HIM *I.e. in a historical work, such as Plutarch's Lives, in which great men are presented in contrasting pairs. The historian Cremutius Cordus, who speaks, means that at one time he had planned to work out such a formal comparison between Germanicus and Alexander.*

143–7 *Jonson expands Tacitus' eulogy of Germanicus to include a scathing counterportrait of Alexander, and caps it with Sabinus' disdainful refusal to compare himself to his own bondman. He then (lines 147–57) expands the praise of Germanicus himself, making it more impassioned, likening him to an imposing roster of recent heroes.*

183 FIFTY SESTERTIA *50,000 sesterces. £375 of our money, notes Jonson marginally—which would be something like $37,000 of ours.*

212–37 *Tacitus, Annals 4.1–2: "Sejanus was born at Vulsinii. His father was a Roman gentleman outside the senate. After increasing his income—it was alleged—by a liaison with a rich debauchee, the boy joined, while still young, the suite of Augustus' grandson Gaius Caesar. Next by various devices he obtained a complete ascendancy over Tiberius. To Sejanus alone the otherwise cryptic emperor spoke freely and unguardedly. This was hardly due to Sejanus' cunning; in that he was outclassed by Tiberius. The cause was rather heaven's anger against Rome—to which the triumph of Sejanus, and his downfall too, were catastrophic. Of audacious character and untiring physique, secretive about himself and ever ready to incriminate others, a blend of arrogance and servility, he concealed behind a carefully modest exterior an unbounded lust for power. Sometimes this impelled him to lavish excesses, but more often to incessant work. And that is as damaging as excess when the throne is its aim.*

*The command of the Guard had hitherto been of slight importance. Sejanus enhanced it by concentrating the Guard battalions, scattered about Rome, in one camp. Orders could reach them simultaneously, and their visible numbers and strength would increase their self-confidence and intimidate the population. His pretexts were, that scattered quarters caused unruliness; that united action would be needed in an emergency; and that a camp away from the temptations of the city would improve discipline. When the camp was ready, he gradually insinuated himself into the men's favour. He would talk with them addressing them by name. And he chose their company- and battalion-commanders himself. Senators' ambitions, too, he tempted with the offices and governorships that were available for his dependants"* (Grant, pp. 153–54). *One may note, again, how Jonson has transformed Tacitus' tone of judicious reporting into one of savage contempt, by the use of epithets such as "abused," and by the climactic final line (216) in which Arruntius invents a more lurid role for Sejanus than anything indicated in Tacitus. On the other hand, Jonson suppresses Tacitus' reference to the freedom with which Tiberius unburdened himself to his favorite, and Tacitus' explanation of Sejanus' ascendancy as a result of "heaven's anger against Rome."*

215 FAT APICIUS *The most celebrated epicure of antiquity, who killed himself through fear of starvation on discovering that of his original fortune only 100,000 pounds remained.*

244–6 *Briggs quotes Coleridge on this passage: "The anachronic mixture in this Arruntius of the Roman republican, to whom Tiberius must have appeared as much a tyrant as Sejanus with his James-and-Charles-the-First zeal for legitimacy of descent in this passage, is amusing. Of our great names, Milton was, I think, the first who could properly be called a republican" (Works, ed. Shedd, 4, 190). The same problem occurs in IV.163–70, with Sabinus, and by implication throughout. Jonson is not, in fact, a sophisticated political theorist or, indeed, a political theorist at all. He clings to a few ethical maxims, such as that which views virtuous governors as good governors irrespective of the particular form of government.*

261–374 *This scene takes place most naturally on an upper level, that of the first gallery. The opening line, "Here he will instant be," points to a place other than the main platform, where Eudemus may await Sejanus in private. Throughout the scene between them, the Germanican partisans remain on the main stage; nothing is said of their departure, and they must be on hand for the arrival of Tiberius. The problem comes at line 374, when attention shifts from Sejanus, soliloquizing above, to Tiberius, rejecting the flatteries of "one [who] kneels to him" on the platform below. Where does Sejanus listen to Tiberius' answer in 375–8? Where is he when he makes his*

*admiring comment in 379? Almost certainly still above, for otherwise he*
*would not have a moment in which to scramble down to the main stage. On*
*the other hand, once having delivered line 379, he would have, until line 503,*
*a long interval in which to descend and reappear. But if the scene was in fact*
*staged this way, it represents an anomaly, since prior to Tiberius' entrance,*
*the upper level has not been understood as forming a continuous space with*
*the platform but rather a separate private apartment, where conversations*
*could take place in seclusion.*

331–2 VAIN . . . GAIN *The use of rhymed couplets at moments like these con-*
*stitutes an auditory form of "gnomic pointing." It makes the aphorism heard*
*distinctly as a separate unit, makes it ring out emphatically, and so heightens*
*the aphoristic effect.*

375–8 WE NOT . . . GODS *From Suetonius,* Life of Tiberius *27: "He so loathed*
*flattery that he would not allow any senator to approach his litter, either to*
*pay his respects or on business, and when an ex-consul in apologizing to him*
*attempted to embrace his knees, he drew back in such haste that he fell over*
*backward. In fact, if anyone in conversation or in a set speech spoke of him*
*in too flattering terms, he did not hesitate to interrupt him, to take him to*
*task, and to correct his language on the spot" (J. C. Rolfe, trans.,* Works,
Loeb Classics, *1 [London, 1914], 335).*

383 COTTA *I adopt Briggs's (and Herford and Simpson's) plausible conjecture (9,*
*603) that Cotta (COT.), one of Sejanus' toadies, is meant to be the speaker*
*here, rather than Cordus (COR.), an enemy to Tiberius who comments*
*scathingly on his duplicity only a few seconds later (line 394).*

385–8 *"The sense is: It is the most refined sort of concerted trickery known to*
*have your own (private) parasite redeem the reputation that you lose out of*
*public subtlety. Sejanus by uttering [line 379], which the politic Tiberius*
*pretended not to hear, made up for the loss which the latter sustained in*
*refusing the flattery addressed to him by Haterius" (Briggs, p. 216).*

454–502 *From Tacitus,* Annals *4.37–38: "This was the time when Farther*
*Spain sent a delegation to the senate, applying to follow Asia's example and*
*build a shrine to Tiberius and his mother. Disdainful of compliment, Tiberius*
*saw an opportunity to refute rumours of his increasing self-importance. 'I am*
*aware, senators,' he said, 'that my present opposition has been widely*
*regarded as inconsistent with my acquiescence in a similar proposal by the*
*cities of Asia. So I will justify both my silence on that occasion and my*
*intentions from now onwards.*

'The divine Augustus did not refuse a temple at Pergamum to himself and the City of Rome. So I, who regard his every action and word as law, followed the precedent thus established—the more readily since the senate was to be worshipped together with myself. One such acceptance may be pardonable. But to have my statue worshipped among the gods in every province would be presumptuous and arrogant. Besides, the honour to Augustus will be meaningless if it is debased by indiscriminate flattery. As for myself, senators, I emphasize to you that I am human, performing human tasks, and content to occupy the first place among men.

'That is what I want later generations to remember. They will do more than justice to my memory if they judge me worthy of my ancestors, careful of your interests, steadfast in danger and fearless of animosities incurred in the public service. Those are my temples in your hearts, those my finest and most lasting images. Marble monuments, if the verdict of posterity is unfriendly, are mere neglected sepulchres. So my requests to provincials and Roman citizens, and heaven, are these. To heaven—grant me, until I die, a peaceful mind and an understanding of what is due to gods and men. To mortals— when I am dead, remember my actions and my name kindly and favourably' "
(Grant, pp. 171–72).

503 ORACLES ARE CEASED *The line contains a veiled anachronism, since the real force of Sejanus' praise lies in the implied comparison of Tiberius to Christ, whose coming was popularly believed, during the Renaissance, to have brought about the cessation of the oracles.*

511–3 *Tacitus, Annals 3.72:* "At about this time Marcus Aemilius Lepidus (IV) asked the senate's leave to strengthen and beautify, at his own expense, the Hall that was the family monument of the Aemilii. For public munificence was still fashionable. Augustus had allowed enemy spoils, or great resources, to be devoted to the adornment of Rome for the applause of posterity. Now Lepidus, though of moderate means, followed their example by repairing his family memorial. When, however, the Theatre of Pompey was accidentally burnt down, Tiberius undertook to rebuild it himself on the grounds that no Pompeius had the means to do so; but its name was to remain unchanged.

*Tiberius commended Sejanus' energy and watchfulness in preventing the fire from spreading beyond Pompey's Theatre; and the senate voted that his statue be erected there*" (Grant, p. 150).

514–16 CONFINING . . . SISTER *Caius Junius Silanus, a governor of Asia, had been convicted of extortion in office and sentenced to exile on the isle of*

*Gyanos. At the request of his sister, a Vestal priestess, he was sent instead to
the less forbidding island of Cythnos.*

520 POMPEY'S THEATER *Erected by Pompey after his second consulship, in 55 B.C.,
and much admired for its size and splendor. It burned down in 22 A.D., but
Sejanus' energy prevented the fire from spreading to the nearby buildings.
Tiberius rebuilt it, and the Senate, as a gesture of thanks to Sejanus, voted
to place his statue in it.*

548–59 Tacitus, Annals 4.7: "*Moreover, there was an alarming potential
avenger in Drusus, who openly showed his hatred and repeatedly complained
that the emperor, though he had a son, went elsewhere for his collaborator.
Soon, Drusus reflected, the collaborator would be called a colleague—the first
steps of an ambitious career are difficult, but once they are achieved helpers
and partisans emerge. 'Already Sejanus has secured this new camp—where
the Guard are at the disposal of their commander. His statue is to be seen in
Pompey's Theatre. The grandsons of us Drususes will be his grandsons too.
What can we do now except trust his moderation and pray he will be for-
bearing?' Drusus often talked like this and many heard him. But even his
confidences were betrayed by his wife—to her lover*" (Grant, pp. 156–57).

560–75 *Jonson's account of this incident is based on Tacitus. Dio reports it
differently:* "*It appears that Sejanus, puffed up by his power and rank, in
addition to his other overweening behaviour, finally turned against Drusus
and once struck him a blow with his fist. As this gave him reason to fear both
Drusus and Tiberius, and as he felt sure at the same time that if he could
once get the young man out of the way, he could handle the other very easily,
he administered poison to the son through the agency of those in attendance
upon him and of Drusus' wife, whom some call Livilla; for Sejanus was her
paramour.*" *Dio Cassius,* Roman History *57.22, ed. Earnest Cary,
Loeb Classics, 7 (London, 1924), 175.*

575 A CASTOR *Drusus' nickname, taken after a celebrated gladiator of the day
because of his brutal temper, which had once led to his striking a distinguished
knight. See Dio,* History *57.14.*

580–1 WHAT . . . NEW *It is noteworthy that the striking episode, one of the rare
coincidences in the play, is immediately afterward declared not to have
affected the course of events. It has merely changed their name. See above,
Introduction.*

Act II

188 AYE *Herford and Simpson point out that the rhyme would be preserved here by reading* Sir.

234 MORE THAN COMPETITORS *The imperial throne, in principle, was partly elective, like the Danish throne in Hamlet, and Germanicus' sons would have had the right to consider themselves "competitors" for it—legitimate claimants—if by no means "immediate heirs."*

285–95 *Tacitus, Annals 4.18: " With this motive Sejanus attacked Gaius Silius (I) and Titius Sabinus. They both owed their ruin to Germanicus' friendship. Silius had also been head of a great army for seven years, winner of an honorary Triumph in Germany, conqueror of Sacrovir. So his downfall would be the more spectacular and alarming" (Grant, p. 162).*

313–16 AS IF . . . SUCH *A grim irony on Jonson's part. Tiberius' notion of cosmic order is that law and liberty would prefer to be destroyed by princes rather than be preserved by "wretches."*

342–3 T'EXTOL . . . LADY *Tacitus, Annals 4.7: " To this end Sejanus employed skilful slanderers. Meanwhile Agrippina's closest friends were induced to accentuate her restlessness by malevolent talk" (Grant, p. 159).*

349 YOUR KINDEST FRIEND *Jonson's marginal note identifies her as Mutilia Prisca. Tacitus (4.12) says of Julius Posthumus, "His adulterous liaison with Mutilia Prisca made him a close friend of the Augusta and particularly apt for Sejanus' purposes; for Prisca had great influence over the old lady, whose jealousy she could use against Agrippina her granddaughter by marriage (not by blood as Livilla)" (Grant, p. 159 n).*

361–2 PUB-/LIC *An instance of the run-over word not uncommon in poetry of the early 17th century, though more often met with in nondramatic than dramatic verse.*

369–72 OUR CITY'S . . . PARTY *Taken from Tacitus, Annals 4.17: "Sejanus . . . declared that Rome was split asunder as though there was civil war: people were calling themselves 'Agrippina's party'—the deepening disunity could only be arrested if some of the ringleaders were removed" (Grant, p. 162). An interesting instance of Jonson's taking a detail from one context and placing it in another. In Tacitus, Sejanus issues these warnings to Tiberius directly, in order to stir him to take harsh measures against Germanicus' sons. Here he more craftily and circuitously sends them to the emperor through two intermediaries, one of them the emperor's still influential mother.*

Act III

5 YOUR . . . HIS "*In ancient Rome, where there was no class of professional advocates taking fees, and where any citizen might come forward as prosecutor or defender, cases of collusions were not infrequent. Hence Roman writers often lay stress on the personal hostility of the prosecutor as a proof of his sincerity*" (Herford and Simpson, 9, 611).

11–12 AND . . . TREASON *Under Tiberius, criminal accusations of every sort gradually came to include the more damning charge of treason* (Tacitus, Annals 3.38). *Silius' trial illustrates the phenomenon* (see below, line 190).

35–81 Tacitus, Annals 4.8: "*All through his son's illness, Tiberius attended the senate. Either he was unalarmed or he wanted to display his will-power. Even when Drusus was dead, and his body awaiting burial, Tiberius continued to attend. The consuls sat on ordinary benches as a sign of mourning. But he reminded them of their dignity and rank. The senators wept. But he silenced them with a consoling oration. 'I know,' he said, 'that I may be criticized for appearing before the senate while my affliction is still fresh. Most mourners can hardly bear even their families' condolences—can hardly look upon the light of day. And that need not be censured as weakness. I, however, have sought sterner solace. The arms into which I have thrown myself are those of the State.'*

*After referring sorrowfully to the Augusta's great age, his grandson's immaturity, and his own declining years, he said that the sons of Germanicus were his only consolation in his grief; and he requested that they should be brought in. The consuls went out, reassured the boys, and conducted them before Tiberius. He took them by the hand, and addressed the senate. 'When these boys lost their father,' he said, 'I entrusted them to their uncle, and begged him—although he had children of his own—to treat them as though they were his blood, and, for posterity's sake, to fashion them after himself. Now Drusus has gone. So my plea is addressed to you. The gods and our country are its witnesses.*

*'Senators: on my behalf as well as your own, adopt and guide these youths, whose birth is so glorious—these great-grandchildren of Augustus. Nero and Drusus Caesars: these senators will take the place of your parents. For, in the station to which you are born, the good and bad in you is of national concern'*" (Grant, p. 157). Jonson, it may be noticed, has heightened Tiberius' eloquence, adding, for example, the figure of the *suns of joy* and *floods of grief* in lines 62–3, and returning to it even more elaborately in 99–105. Jonson's more learned auditors would have measured Tiberius' hypocrisy

> *not only by the comments of the upright bystanders but in the light of his subsequent treatment of the princes: he starved them to death, in conditions of the utmost cruelty (see Tacitus, 6.23–24).*

113–27 Tacitus, *Annals 4.8–9:* " *These words were greeted by loud weeping among the senators, followed by heartfelt prayers for the future. Indeed, if Tiberius had stopped there, he would have left his audience sorry for him and proud of their responsibility. But by reverting to empty discredited talk about restoring the Republic and handing the government to the consuls or others, he undermined belief even in what he had said sincerely and truthfully*" (Grant, pp. 157–58).

154 AFER *One of Jonson's infrequent departures from rigorous historicity. Afer prosecuted other accused citizens at about this time, but not Silius.*

170–1 HAVE I . . . FOR *Tacitus makes it clear that the law entitling informers to the property of their victims (if the latter were convicted, as they usually were) helped foster a class of professional stool-pigeons, skilled at trumping up accusations against those whose wealth they coveted. See Annals 3.28; 4.30, 36; Dio, History 58.4.8; and Suetonius, Tiberius 61.*

181–90 Tacitus, *Annals 4.19:* " *The prosecution developed its case—longstanding connivance with Sacrovir and cognizance of his rebellion; victory ruined by rapacity. Silius' wife was charged as an accomplice. In extortion they were undoubtedly both involved. But the case was conducted as a treason trial*" (Grant, pp. 162–63).

190 THOU LIEST *Strictly speaking, and at a pinch, this defiant giving of the lie might be construed to refer only to Afer's final charge, that of treason. In this sense Jonson may be said to have covered himself against the imputation of altering history. In fact, of course, no one watching the scene could possibly avoid concluding that all of Afer's charges were lies and forgeries.*

197–208 Tacitus, *Annals 4.19:* " *When accused, Silius requested a brief adjournment until the accuser's consulship should end. But Tiberius opposed this arguing that officials often proceeded against private citizens, and that there must be no limitation of the rights of the consuls, on whose watchfulness it depended 'that the State takes no harm.' It was typical of Tiberius to use antique terms to veil new sorts of villainy*" (Grant, p. 162).

272–8, 288–91, 305–8 Tacitus, *Annals 4.18:* " *Many thought that he had aggravated his offence by imprudence. For he had boasted excessively of his own army's unbroken loyalty when others had lapsed into mutiny.' If the revolt* had spread to my brigades,' he said, 'Tiberius could not have kept the throne.' The emperor felt that these assertions of an obligation beyond all recompense damaged his own position. For services are welcome as long as it seems possible to repay them, but when they greatly exceed that point they produce not gratitude but hatred" (Grant, p. 162). In Jonson, Afer waxes vastly more detailed on the subject of Silius' vaunting than in Tacitus, so that he impresses one strongly as acting from personal spite. In 305–6 Jonson transfers Tacitus' comment on the ingratitude of princes to Silius himself, making it part of a direct confrontation of Tiberius. The whole passage makes remarkable dramatic use of what, in the source, does not seem like especially dramatic material.

275  YOURS Afer, in the Quarto, uses the second person singular forms—"thou," "thy," "thine"—throughout. Editors have noted with some puzzlement that in the Folio text he shifts to plural forms beginning at line 275. I am indebted to Miss Moneera Doss for the acute suggestion that Jonson is attempting in this manner to distinguish between direct address and indirect discourse.

303  DOUBTFUL PRINCES Editors have conjectured that the original reading of this line gave offence to the authorities, and formed one item in the bill of complaints against Jonson, as a result of which, in revising the play for the Folio, he decided to make the accusation against princes somewhat less sweeping.

355–69 Tacitus, Annals 4.20: "Never before had Tiberius gone to such pains regarding other men's property. Gaius Asinius Gallus proposed Sosia's banishment, moving that half of her property should be confiscated and the other half left to her children. Marcus Aemilius Lepidus (IV), however, counter-proposed that a quarter should go to the accusers—as the law required —but that her children should have the rest.

I find that this Marcus Lepidus played a wise and noble part in events. He often palliated the brutalities caused by other people's sycophancy. And he had a sense of proportion—for he enjoyed unbroken influence and favour with Tiberius. This compels me to doubt whether, like other things, the friendships and enmities of rulers depend on destiny and the luck of a man's birth. Instead, may not our personalities play some part, enabling us to steer a way, safe from intrigues and hazards, between perilous insubordination and degrading servility?" (Grant, p. 163). The Tacitean passage on Lepidus is reproduced intact here, so that the reader may see what Jonson left out: first, the fact of Lepidus' "unbroken influence and favour with Tiberius," and second, the probably (to Jonson) unsatisfactory speculation over the "friendships and enmities of rulers." If there is one thing Jonson will not allow in

Sejanus, *it is friendship between a good man like Lepidus and a brutal, degenerate tyrant like Tiberius.*

379–406 Tacitus, Annals 4.34: " *The following year began with the prosecution of Aulus Cremutius Cordus on a new and previously unheard-of charge: praise of Brutus in his* History, *and the description of Cassius as 'the last of the Romans.' The prosecutors were dependants of Sejanus; that was fatal to the accused man. So was the grimness of Tiberius' face as he listened to the defence*" (Grant, p. 169).

407–60 *This is the speech referred to by Drummond of Hawthornden:* "In his *Sejanus he hath translated a whole oration of Tacitus*" (Conversations, 602). *Tacitus, Annals 4.34–35:* "'*Senators, my words are blamed. My actions are not blameworthy. Nor were these words of mine aimed against the emperor or his parent, to whom the law of treason applies. I am charged with praising Brutus and Cassius. Yet many have written of their deeds— always with respect. Livy, outstanding for objectivity as well as eloquence, praised Pompey so warmly that Augustus called him* "the Pompeian." *But their friendship did not suffer. And Livy never called Cassius and Brutus bandits and parricides—their fashionable designations today. He described them in language appropriate to distinguished men.*

'*Gaius Asinius Pollio (I) gave a highly complimentary account of them. Marcus Valerius Messalla Corvinus (I) called Cassius* "my commander." *Both lived out wealthy and honoured lives. When Cicero praised Cato to the skies, the dictator Julius Caesar reacted by writing a speech against him—as in a lawsuit. Antony's letters, Brutus' speeches, contain scathing slanders against Augustus. The poems of Marcus Furius Bibaculus and Catullus— still read—are crammed with insults against the Caesars. Yet the divine Julius, the divine Augustus endured them and let them be. This could well be interpreted as wise policy, and not merely forbearance. For things unnoticed are forgotten; resentment confers status upon them.*

'*I am not speaking of the Greeks. For they left licence unpunished as well as freedom—or, at most, words were countered by words. But among us, too, there has always been complete, uncensored liberty to speak about those whom death has placed beyond hatred or partiality. Cassius and Brutus are not in arms at Philippi now. I am not on the platform inciting the people to civil war. They died seventy years ago! They are known by their statues— even the conqueror did not remove them. And they have their place in the historian's pages. Posterity gives everyone his due honour. If I am con-*

*demned, people will remember me as well as Cassius and Brutus'"* (*Grant,* pp. *169–70*).

427–8 HEAVED UP ... HEAV'N *This translates Tacitus'* "*Catonem caelo aequavit*" *with exceptional expressive energy.*

440–1 SUPPRESSED ... CONFESSED *The couplet brings Cordus' speech to an intermediary cadence, and confers epigrammatic weight on one of its central themes.*

471–80 *Tacitus, Annals 4.35:* "*Cremutius walked out of the senate, and starved himself to death. The senate ordered his books to be burnt by the aediles. But they survived, first hidden and later republished. This makes one deride the stupidity of people who believe that today's authority can destroy tomorrow's memories. On the contrary, repressions of genius increase its prestige. All that tyrannical conquerors, and imitators of their brutalities, achieve is their own disrepute and their victims' renown*" (*Grant, p. 170*).

503–76 *Tacitus, Annals 4.39–40:* "*Sejanus' judgement now became affected by too great success; and feminine ambition hustled him, since Livilla was demanding her promised marriage. He wrote a memorandum to the emperor. (It was customary at that time to address him in writing even when he was at Rome.) This is what Sejanus said:*

'*The kindness of your father Augustus, and your own numerous marks of favour, have accustomed me to bringing my hopes and desires to the imperial ear as readily as to the gods. I have never asked for brilliant office. I would rather watch and work, like any soldier, for the emperor's safety. Yet I have gained the greatest privilege—to be thought worthy of a marriage-link with your house. That inspired me to hope: besides, I have heard that Augustus, when marrying his daughter, had considered even gentlemen outside the senate. So please bear in mind, if you should seek a husband for Livilla, your friend who would gain nothing but prestige from the relationship. For I am content with the duties I have to perform; satisfied—for my children's sake—if my family is safeguarded against the unfounded malevolence of Agrippina. For myself, to live my appointed span under so great an emperor is all the life I desire.*'

*In reply Tiberius praised Sejanus' loyalty, touched lightly on his own favours to him, and asked for time, ostensibly for unbiased reflection. Finally, he answered. '*Other men's decisions,*' he wrote, '*may be based on their own interests, but rulers are situated differently, since in important matters they need to consider public opinion. So I do not resort to the easy answer, that*

> Livilla can decide for herself whether she should fill Drusus' place by re-
> marrying, or stay in the same home. Nor will I reply that she has a mother
> and grandmother who are her more intimate advisers than myself. I will be
> more frank. In the first place Agrippina's ill-feelings will be greatly intensified
> if Livilla marries: this would virtually split the imperial house in two. Even
> now, the women's rivalry is irrepressible, and my grandsons are torn between
> them. What if the proposed marriage accentuated the feud?
>
> 'You are mistaken, Sejanus, if you think that Livilla, once married to
> Gaius Caesar and then to Drusus, would be content to grow old as the wife
> of a gentleman outside the senate—or that you could retain your present rank.
> Even if I allowed it, do you think it would be tolerated by those who have
> seen her brother and father, and our ancestors, holding the great office of state?
> You do not want to rise above your present rank. But the officials and dis-
> tinguished men who force their way in upon you and consult you on all
> matters maintain openly that you have long ago eclipsed other non-senators
> and risen above any friend of my father's. Moreover, envying you, they
> criticize me.
>
> 'Augustus, you say, considered marrying his daughter to a gentleman out-
> side the senate. But he foresaw that the man set apart by such an alliance would
> be enormously elevated; and is it surprising, therefore, that those he had in
> mind were men like Gaius Proculeius, noted for their retiring abstention from
> public affairs? Besides, if we are noting Augustus' delay in making up his
> mind, the decisive consideration is that the sons-in-law whom he actually
> chose were Marcus Agrippa and then, in due course, myself. I have spoken
> openly, as your friend. However, what you and Livilla decide, I shall not
> oppose. Of certain projects of my own, and additional ties by which I plan to
> link you with me, I shall not speak now. This only shall I say: for your
> merits and your devotion to me, no elevation would be too high. When the
> time comes to speak before the senate and public, I shall not be silent' "
> (Grant, pp. 172–73).

514 WORTHY HIS ALLIANCE *This refers to an episode of 20 A.D., when Tiberius
arranged for Sejanus' infant daughter to be betrothed to the infant son of
the future emperor Claudius, a member of the royal family. See Suetonius,
Claudius 5.27.*

530 ff. *Jonson makes Tiberius' answer even more devious and wily than it had in
fact been. Where the historical Tiberius "refuses to resort to" a glib reply
concerning Livia, declines to say that "she has a mother and a grandmother*

*to advise her," Jonson's Tiberius makes precisely these replies at first, and
then proceeds to disavow them.*

560–4 THE STATE . . . THEE *A good instance of Jonson's flair for converting his
material into vivid dramatic speech. All the expressive characterizing force
of the passage, in the idiomatic verbs "stick not," "murmur," "upbraid,"
etc., and in the resumption of one of the key metaphors of the play, that of
climbing, in lines 562–3, is Jonson's contribution.*

603–20 Tacitus, Annals 4.41: *"he turned his attention to persuading Tiberius
to settle in some attractive place far from Rome. He foresaw many advantages
in this. He himself would control access to the emperor—as well as most of his
correspondence, since it would be transmitted by Guardsmen. Besides, the
ageing monarch, slackening in retirement, would soon be readier to delegate
governmental functions. Meanwhile Sejanus himself would become less un-
popular when his large receptions ceased—by eliminating inessentials, he
would strengthen his real power. So he increasingly denounced to Tiberius
the drudgeries of Rome, its crowds and innumerable visitors, and spoke
warmly of peace and solitude, far from vexation and friction: where first
things could come first"* (Grant, p. 174).

637–46 Briggs (pp. 251–52) quotes appositely from Machiavelli's Discorsi, III,
6: *"A Prince therefore who wishes to guard himself from congiure should
more fear those to whom he has done too many favours than those whom he
has done too many injuries; for the latter lack opportunity, the former have
it; and the will is the same, since the desire to dominate is as great or greater
than the desire for revenge. They should therefore give only so much authority
to their friends as still leaves some distance, and as allows something in
between to be coveted, otherwise it will be a rare thing if he will not [place]
them among the first [on the proscribed list]."*

714–49 *Macro is conceived as an arch-Machiavel, and the present soliloquy, in
which he affirms his dedication to his trade of princes' creature, might stand
as one version of the Machiavel's Creed, comparable to that of Richard of
Gloucester in Shakespeare's 3 Henry VI, III.2.165–95. Richard stresses
dissembling as his prime asset, Macro his ability to stifle human feeling in
himself.*

### Act IV

47–60 Tacitus, Annals 4.59: *"A dangerous accident to Tiberius at this time
stimulated idle gossip, and gave him reason for increased confidence in
Sejanus' friendship and loyalty. While they were dining at a villa called The*

Cave, in a natural cavern between the sea at Amyclae and the hills of Fundi, there was a fall of rock at the cave-mouth. Several servants were crushed, and amid the general panic the diners fled. But Sejanus braced himself across Tiberius on hands and knees, keeping off the falling boulders. That is how the soldiers who rescued them found him. The incident increased Sejanus' power. Tiberius believed him disinterested and listened trustingly to his advice, however disastrous" (Grant, p. 182).

93–232 Tacitus, Annals 4.68–70: "The next year began deplorably. A distinguished gentleman outside the senate called Titius Sabinus was dragged to gaol because he had been Germanicus' friend. Sabinus had maintained every attention to Germanicus' widow and children, visiting their home, escorting them in public—of their crowds of followers he was the only survivor. Decent men respected this, but spiteful people hated him. His downfall was planned by four ex-praetors ambitious for the consulship. For the only access to this lay through Sejanus, and only crimes secured Sejanus' goodwill.

The four arranged that, with the others present as witnesses, one of them, Lucanius Latiaris (who knew Sabinus slightly), should trap him with a view to prosecution. So Latiaris after some casual remarks complimented Sabinus on his unshaken adherence, in its misfortunes, to the family he had supported in its prosperity—and he commented respectfully about Germanicus, sympathetically about Agrippina. Sabinus burst into tearful complaints; for misery is demoralizing. Latiaris then openly attacked Sejanus as cruel, domineering, and ambitious—and did not even spare Tiberius. These exchanges of forbidden confidences seemed to cement a close friendship. So now Sabinus sought out Latiaris' company, frequenting his house and unburdening his sorrows to this outwardly reliable companion.

The four partners next considered how to make these conversations available to a larger audience. The meeting-place had to appear private. Even if they stood behind the doors, they risked being seen or heard or detected by some chance suspicion. So the three senators wedged themselves between roof and ceiling. In this hiding-place—as undignified as the trick was despicable—they applied their ears to chinks and holes. Meanwhile Latiaris had found Sabinus out of doors and, pretending to have fresh news to report, escorted him home to Sabinus' bedroom. There Latiaris dwelt on the unfailing subject of past and present distresses, introducing some fresh terrors too. Sabinus embroidered at greater length on the same theme: once grievances find expression, there is no silencing them. Acting rapidly, the accusers wrote to Tiberius and disclosed the history of the trap and their own *deplorable role. At Rome there was unprecedented agitation and terror. People behaved secretively even to their intimates, avoiding encounters and conversation, shunning the ears both of friends and strangers. Even voiceless, inanimate objects—ceilings and walls—were scanned suspiciously.*

*In a letter read in the senate on January 1st Tiberius, after the customary New Year formalities, rounded upon Sabinus, alleging that he had tampered with certain of the emperor's ex-slaves and plotted against his life. The letter unequivocally demanded retribution. This was hastily decreed. The condemned man was dragged away, crying (as loudly as the cloak muffling his mouth and the noose round his neck allowed) that this was a fine New Year ceremony—this year's sacrifice was to Sejanus"* (Grant, pp. 186–87).

95 BETWEEN . . . CEILING *The staging of this scene is a problem. Do Rufus and Opsius mount into the hut at line 115, by means of a rope ladder, as Herford and Simpson suggest (9, 621)? This would be extremely awkward. Or do they, as Allan Gilbert has proposed ("The Eavesdroppers in* Sejanus," *Modern Language Notes, 69 [1954], 166), simply "appl[y] their ears to holes and cracks," in accord with the indications in Tacitus? This seems likely, but it leaves unanswered the question of their whereabouts on stage throughout the scene. "Between the roof and ceiling" implies that they are above Sabinus and Latiaris during the interview between the latter, but if so—if they are above in the gallery—they have barely a moment, after Opsius' cry at line 217, in which to descend and "lay hands upon the traitor" along with their fellow spy. William A. Armstrong, "Ben Jonson and Jacobean Stagecraft," in* Jacobean Theatre, Stratford-upon-Avon Studies, *1 (London, 1960), 53, thinks it likely that the three spies are on the balcony when Latiaris gives his order at line 95, that the other two then conceal themselves "by lying behind the balcony rails while Latiaris and Sabinus [talk] below," "that they [jump] to the platform" when the time comes to arrest Sabinus—and that the whole episode has been needlessly complicated in its staging by Jonson's insistence on following Tacitus. See above, discussion of a somewhat similar problem in N. I.261–374.*

110 ALLIED TO HIM *Latiaris, who in Tacitus is only an acquaintance of Sabinus, is made a cousin by Jonson. This intensifies the odium of the betrayal.*

127 THEY . . . WE *The stoicism and reserve of Sabinus here contrast strikingly with his behavior in Tacitus—his instant giving way to tears, his subsequent self-indulgence in complaint.*

140–1 SPIES . . . EYES *The dramatic irony is devastating. Sabinus, as the audience very well knows, is a victim of the thing he is describing, in the very*

> *moment in which he describes it. As he talks, he is being transfixed by*
> *Latiaris' murdering eye.*

175 RHODES *Tiberius had lived in retirement on Rhodes during part of Augustus'*
*reign, but at the moment of this dialogue he was on Capri.*

228–9 THE YEAR . . . SEJANUS *Jonson, following Tacitus, makes the arrest of*
*Sabinus occur on the New Year. As the New Year was a sacred festival, the*
*proceedings have the added quality of a desecration.*

285–7 *The incident of Sabinus' dog, taken from Dio (History 58.1), appears*
*also in Sir Thomas Elyot, in* The Governor, II.13, *under "Ingratitude*
*and the dispraise thereof," as an illustration of the kind of gratitude that men*
*ought to feel, but rarely do.*

293–8 *Briggs (p. 260) aptly observes that "the words of Lepidus are not quite*
*consistent with the historical facts, since, as Tacitus tells us, he enjoyed the*
*constant favor of Tiberius." Jonson, of course, does not show Tiberius*
*actively persecuting or in any way molesting Lepidus. He simply eliminates*
*all mention of good will between them. See above, N. III.355–69, and*
*Introduction.*

380–6 *Tacitus,* Annals *6.21: "When seeking occult guidance Tiberius would*
*retire to the top of his house, with a single tough, illiterate ex-slave as*
*confidant. Those astrologers whose skill Tiberius had decided to test were*
*escorted to him by this man over pathless, precipitous ground; for the house*
*overhung a cliff. Then, on their way down, if they were suspected of un-*
*reliability or fraudulence, the ex-slave hurled them into the sea below, so*
*that no betrayer of the secret proceedings should survive" (Grant, pp. 204–05).*
*Jonson aggravates the charge against Tiberius by altering his motive for*
*hurling men into the sea, making it not suspicion, or fear, but envy.*

391–401 *Tacitus,* Annals *6.1: "Free-born children were his victims. He was*
*fascinated by beauty, youthful innocence, and aristocratic birth. New names*
*for types of perversion were invented. Slaves were charged to locate and*
*procure his requirements. They rewarded compliance, overbore reluctance*
*with menaces, and—if resisted by parents or relations—kidnapped their*
*victims, and violated them on their own account. It was like the sack of a*
*captured city" (Grant, p. 195).*

410–514 *The manuscripts of Tacitus break off at about this point, and do not*
*pick up the thread until after Sejanus' overthrow, two years later. Jonson*
*fills in the crucial gap in his story with borrowings from Dio Cassius. The*
*present passage comes from History 58.6: "Tiberius . . . who was no*

*longer ignorant of anything that concerned his minister, was planning how he might put him to death; but, not finding any way of doing this openly and safely, he handled both Sejanus himself and the Romans in general in a remarkable fashion, so as to learn exactly what was in their minds. He kept sending despatches of all kinds regarding himself both to Sejanus and to the senate, now saying that he was in a bad state of health and almost at the point of death, and now that he was exceedingly well and would arrive in Rome directly. At one moment he would heartily praise Sejanus, and again would as heartily denounce him; and, while honouring some of Sejanus' friends out of regard for him, he would be disgracing others"* (Cary, 7, 203).

Further indebtedness to Dio occurs below in V.25–210, the scene of Sejanus' omens and sacrifices (Dio, 58.5, 7); in V.431–74, the account of the senators crowding in on Sejanus and fawning on him (Dio, 58.5); in the reading of Tiberius' letter, with the reactions of the senators and the arrest of Sejanus, V.543–736 (Dio, 58.9–11); and in the part of the final narration dealing with Apicata, V.856–77 (Dio, 58.11).

438 POLLUX . . . HERCULES *These two oaths "replace an original 'Castor' and 'Pollux' found in the Quarto and the first state of the 1616 Folio; the corrections were made in the proof by Jonson. . . . Jonson did not know at first that 'Castor' was a woman's oath, and 'Hercules' a man's"* (Herford and Simpson, 9, 624. See also the textual note to Sejanus, Herford and Simpson, 4, 336–37).

## Act V

25–93 Jonson, in order to stress the element of hubristic defiance in Sejanus, makes him more of a blasphemer and skeptic than he actually was. Dio tells of his rituals, his taking of auspices, his perturbation upon learning of the snake in the statue, and his offering of sacrifices to offset bad omens (History 58.5–7).

117–70 It is hard to discover much point to Regulus' comings and goings in this scene, or to Macro's sarcasms on them. They would seem to be a rare instance of Jonson's hamming his material so as to make it more palatable for the stage.

307 SOME ROOM *The gallery, where the interview with Macro (lines 323–99) takes place. Of the three scenes in the play that seem to require an upper level, this is the only one that presents no staging difficulties. See above, N. I.261–374 and N. IV.95.*

363 TRIBUNICIAL DIGNITY "*Giving Sejanus the tribunitial power was equivalent to declaring him heir to the throne, as from a constitutional point of view, the emperor's authority rested largely upon it; the important point was that it carried with it the right of veto and of interference in state business, and made the holder's person sacrosanct*" (Briggs, p. 276).

604–6 Jonson uses here some phrases from a later letter of Tiberius quoted by Suetonius and Tacitus: "'*If I know what to write to you at this time, senators,' he said, 'or how to write it, or what not to write, may heaven plunge me into a worse ruin than I feel overtaking me every day!*'" Upon which Tacitus comments, "*His crimes and wickednesses had rebounded to torment himself*" (Annals 6.6; Grant, p. 197). Jonson, by the omission of the latter half of the sentence, and by the altered context in which he places the letter, transforms it from an expression of "*the intolerable anguish of a guilty mind*" (Gifford, quoted in Briggs, p. 283), to another masterly stroke of dissimulation and affected hesitation on Tiberius' part.

696–832 Jonson's account of the violence and hysteria of the mob (lines 696–804) comes from Juvenal's Tenth Satire, lines 56–107; Claudian's In Rufinum, with its description of the dismemberment of Rufinus, supplies in part the basis for lines 814–32.

818 MOUNTING This word is so inappropriate, so nearly unintelligible, in context, that editors have suspected textual corruption, but no satisfactory emendation has been proposed.

834 THERE . . . PITY Among numerous echoes of Jonson, and of Sejanus in particular, in the plays of Webster, editors have infrequently mentioned the present line, imitated in a similar context in The Duchess of Malfi, IV.2.272, when Bosola shows the bodies of the Duchess' children to Duke Ferdinand.

839–54 Tacitus, Annals 5.9: "*The general rage against Sejanus was now subsiding, appeased by the executions already carried out. Yet retribution was now decreed against his remaining children. They were taken to prison. The boy understood what lay ahead of him. But the girl uncomprehendingly repeated: 'What have I done? Where are you taking me? I will not do it again!' She could be punished with a beating, she said, like other children. Contemporary writers report that, because capital punishment of a virgin was unprecedented, she was violated by the executioner, with the noose beside her. Then both were strangled, and their young bodies thrown on to the Gemonian Steps*" (Grant, p. 194). Jonson accentuates both the vividness *and the pathos of the account in Tacitus. He dwells more fully first on the innocence of the children, then on the cruelty of Macro and the brutality of the hangman. In one respect he makes the incident less horrible: he puts it down to the continuing fury of the populace, whereas in Tacitus it is cold-bloodedly " decreed" despite an abatement of the general rage. On the whole, though, Jonson stresses the insensate savagery of the crime, and invokes pity for the innocent victims, as distinct from their father, whom we are expressly advised (lines 893–7) not to pity.*

858–77 *The description of Apicata's despair far outdoes in turbulence and grandeur the brief mention of it in Dio (History 58.11), where she is said simply to have gone away, after viewing her children's bodies, in order to compose her statement concerning Drusus' death. Jonson makes the scene a final off-stage climax to the terrible events of the day, conferring on the bereaved Apicata some of the towering passion of a Hecuba or a Medea.*

# Appendix: The Text

*Sejanus* was first acted in 1603, entered on the Stationers' Register in 1604, and printed by Thomas Thorp in 1605, in an extremely accurate text. The exactness of the marginal annotations, the closeness with which the typography conveyed Jonson's metrical intentions, and the corrections made in proof, all suggest that Jonson oversaw the printing himself. But although the Quarto constitutes an authoritative text, it is superseded by that of the 1616 Folio, which was revised by Jonson in about eighty places as the volume was going through the press.

The present edition attempts to present a modernized version of the Folio text, and to record the main variations between Folio and Quarto. Modernization, while it makes a text more usable for modern readers, involves its penalties, especially in the realm of punctuation. Present-day punctuation tends to be lighter than that of Jonson's day, and modernizing often leads to a loss, or a blurring, of Jonson's caesural effects. A line cited by Herford and Simpson in connection with the change from Quarto to Folio may serve to illustrate. Tiberius, replying to Sejanus' request for the hand of his daughter-in-law Livia, says, in the Folio:

> We cannot but commend thy pietie,
> Most-lou'd SEIANVS, in acknowledging
> Those bounties; which we, faintly, such remember. [III.530–2]

Herford and Simpson observe: "The Quarto prints, 'Those, bounties,' Tiberius affecting modesty: 'Those—well, call them bounties if you like'" (4, 342). Something, that is, has been lost dramatically by the dropping of the comma after "Those." Something has also been added, a new stroke of hesitancy: the comma before "faintly," which again suggests that Tiberius is affecting delicacy, pretending not to remember his own bounties too vividly. The new comma can be reproduced, at need, in a modernized text; the original one cannot. It was, of course, lost in the transit from Quarto to Folio; Jonson himself allowed it to happen. But such expressive details of pointing are the rule rather than the exception in his texts, and a modernized edition cannot preserve more than a fraction of them, hence cannot convey more than a shadow of the heavy rhetorical punctuation favored by Jonson himself. Ideally, his plays should be read in the texts he designed for them. The present edition, then, is not intended to supplant the original (or a close scholarly reprint of it), but to lead the reader toward it.

Punctuation being lightened to conform to modern practice, the old gnomic pointing—the use of quotation marks to call attention to aphorisms or sententious remarks—has been eliminated. On the other hand, elisions and contractions have been retained so as not to upset Jonson's metrical arrangements. Retained for the same reason are the metrical apostrophes with which Jonson indicates a slight slurring of two adjacent syllables, as in I.121–2:

> Sabinus and myself
> Had means to know'him within, and can report him.

A few such metrical apostrophes, omitted from the Folio, have here been restored on the authority of the Quarto, following the precedent of Herford and Simpson.

The textual notes at the bottom of each page attempt to record (1) all substantive departures from the Folio, and (2) all significant Quarto variants. "Substantive" and "significant," here, mean, effectively, "involving changes of word." Category (1) consists of two sub-categories: (a) places where a Folio reading is corrected by a Quarto reading, and (b) a few places where a reading from both Quarto and Folio has been emended. Most of the latter cases correct obvious errors, and all have the authority of a substantial number of earlier editors. The variants of Category (2) appear not only in the Quarto but usually in an uncorrected state of the Folio as well. This fact has not otherwise been separately noted. Variations in punctuation between Quarto and Folio have not been recorded, nor have variations of spelling, except in rare instances where a new spelling might be construed as making a new word. Jonson's stage directions added in the Folio are of course incorporated into the present text, but the notes do not distinguish these from directions already present in the Quarto. A few other stage directions, especially those indicating asides, have been added editorially, for purposes of clarity, and bracketed. Finally, the extensive marginal notes of the Quarto, in which Jonson cites his sources, have neither been reproduced nor recorded, the page references to sixteenth-century editions making them useful only to scholars wishing to consult those same editions. Interested readers should turn to Herford and Simpson, 4, 472–85.

# Selected Reading List

EDITIONS

*Ben Jonson*, ed. C. H. Herford and Percy and Evelyn Simpson, 11 vols. Oxford, 1925–52. The standard edition of Jonson's complete works. Volumes 1 and 2 contain a biography of Jonson and introductions to the plays (the introduction to *Sejanus* is in Volume 2). The text of *Sejanus* appears in Volume 4, and the commentary in Volume 9.

*Sejanus*, ed. W. Bang, Materialien zur Kunde der älteren Englischen Dramas, Vol. 7, Nos. 1–2, Louvain, 1905–08.

*Sejanus*, ed. W. D. Briggs, Heath Belles Lettres Series, Boston, 1911.

*Seianus His Fall*, ed. Henry de Vocht, from the Quarto of 1605, Materials for the Study of the Old English Drama, New Series, Vol. 11, Louvain, 1935.

CRITICISM

Boughner, Daniel C., "Jonson's Use of Lipsius in *Sejanus*," *Modern Language Notes*, 73 (1958), 247–55.

——— "Juvenal, Horace and *Sejanus*," *Modern Language Notes*, 75 (1960), 545–50.

———"Sejanus and Machiavelli," *Studies in English Literature 1500–1900*, 1, No. 2 (1961), 81–100.

Bryant, Joseph Allen, Jr., "The Nature of the Conflict in Jonson's *Sejanus*," *Vanderbilt Studies in the Humanities*, 1 (1951), 197–219.

——— "The Significance of Ben Jonson's First Requirement for Tragedy: 'Truth of Argument,'" *Studies in Philology*, 49 (1952), 195–213.

Selected Reading List

Bryant, Joseph Allen, Jr., "*Catiline* and the Nature of Jonson's Tragic Fable," *PMLA*, 69 (1954), 265–77; reprinted in Jonas A. Barish, ed. *Ben Jonson: A Collection of Critical Essays* (Englewood Cliffs, N.J., 1963), pp. 147–59.

Burton, K. M., "The Political Tragedies of Chapman and Ben Jonson," *Essays in Criticism*, 2 (1952), 397–412.

Enck, John J., "The Shapes of Dangers," Chap. 5 in *Jonson and the Comic Truth* (Madison, Wisc., 1957), pp. 89–109.

Gilbert, Allan, "The Eavesdroppers in Jonson's *Sejanus*," *Modern Language Notes*, 69 (1954), 164–66.

Hill, Geoffrey, "The World's Proportion: Jonson's Dramatic Poetry in *Sejanus* and *Catiline*," in *Jacobean Theatre*, Stratford-upon-Avon Studies in English, 1 (London, 1960), 113–31.

Honig, Edwin, "*Sejanus* and *Coriolanus*: A Study in Alienation," *Modern Language Quarterly*, 12 (1951), 407–21.

Kirschbaum, Leo, "Jonson, Seneca, and *Mortimer*," in *Studies in Honor of John Wilcox*, ed. A. Dayle Wallace and Woodburn O. Ross (Detroit, 1958), 9–22.

Nash, Ralph, "Jonson's Tragic Poems," *Studies in Philology*, 55 (1958), 164–86.

Ornstein, Robert, "Ben Jonson," Chap. 3 in *The Moral Vision of Jacobean Tragedy* (Madison, Wisc., 1960), pp. 84–104.

Prior, Moody E., *The Language of Tragedy* (New York, 1947), pp. 112–19.

Ricks, Christopher, "*Sejanus* and Dismemberment," *Modern Language Notes*, 76 (1961), 301–08.

THE YALE PAPERBOUNDS